Deeper Life Series

Deeper Life Series

A deeper life in Christ

Betty Guerin

authorHOUSE®

AuthorHouse™
1663 Liberty Drive
Bloomington, IN 47403
www.authorhouse.com
Phone: 1-800-839-8640

Published by AuthorHouse   03/09/2012

ISBN: 978-1-4634-4592-8 (sc)
ISBN: 978-1-4634-4591-1 (e)

Library of Congress Control Number: 2011913812

Any people depicted in stock imagery provided by Thinkstock are models, and such images are being used for illustrative purposes only.
Certain stock imagery © Thinkstock.

This book is printed on acid-free paper.

Because of the dynamic nature of the Internet, any web addresses or links contained in this book may have changed since publication and may no longer be valid. The views expressed in this work are solely those of the author and do not necessarily reflect the views of the publisher, and the publisher hereby disclaims any responsibility for them.

Increasing in our Souls!

Our deeper life purpose today is to increase in our soul.

We must increase in our mind, will, and emotions. When I say we must increase, I mean have a deeper revelation of who Jesus is and what God promised us as we get to know who we are in Him. God promised we would be strong in the Lord because Jesus gave us the power over all the powers of the enemy! (Luke 10:19) God has made us strong so that purpose will be fulfilled in our life time and not defeat. We will finish strong in the Lord. God's plan can not and will not fail!!!

The Purpose for a deeper Life! Psalm 33:11 (New International Version)

¹¹ but the plans of the LORD stand firm forever,
the purposes of his heart through all generations.

The purpose for those who are in the kingdom of God is that we live in the plan of God and have a firm stand in what God said about us, what he said we can and will do. Live the way he said we can live, do what he said we can do, and have what he said we can have! We just have to take that firm stand and don't be moved by what we see in the natural!!!

Psalm 57:2 (New International Version)

² I cry out to God Most High,
to God, who fulfills {his purpose} for me.

Today we must not allow ourselves to live a surface life, a life where we accept anything the world issues out to us. But cry out to God our most high; He is the only one who fulfills his purpose in us. God is the only one who has promised to do it! So, we cannot bow to this world's purpose. We cannot be conformed to this world but transformed by the renewing of our minds.

Now when I say don't bow to this world, I mean the world wants us to bow to its way of doing things and not the way God's word tells us to.

Don't let go of God for anything else that comes into your life. Don't allow your heart and mind to be troubled about the way things are manifesting in the world! Every time it seems like you are watching and listening to everything that is showing up ungodly, just begin to think on those things that are above. Things that are good, lovely and of a good report! When we think about our heavenly position in Jesus Christ, we will remain focused on the things that will keep us stable and fixed in the Lord. Remember your thoughts will and have the ability to take you away from your purpose. So, guard over your mind by thinking heavenly thoughts which God has designed for you and cause you to begin to sow into those things that are good, lovely and of a good report for your mind, will and emotions.

We are leaders striving toward (masteries)—expert skill and expert knowledge processing outstanding abilities—and complete control—having total control over something or somebody.

Proverbs 19:21 (New International Version)

21 Many are the plans in a man's heart,
     but it is the Lord's purpose that prevails.

We have many plans in our heart but the Lord's purpose will always take preeminence. God wants us to be in control over the devil to the point He knows that we are not going to allow him to over power us in this race. We will work together for one common cause and we are not going anywhere with him and we are not going to join his organization.

This means he will not cause us to leave our purpose to be used by the devil. God has given us power over all the power of the enemy; Luke 10:19 assures us we have all of the power over the enemy here in the earth and we are winning in the spirit!

The devil is a liar and a deceiver, but God's word is truth. Jesus is the truth, the way and the life (John 14: 6) and God expect us to have power over the enemy in the church. The church should be the most powerful institution in this whole world. We should be the example of healthiness, lividness, powerfulness, and most gratefulness ever found in the world.

Psalm 138:8 (New International Version)

[8] The LORD will fulfill his purpose for me;
    your love, O LORD, endures forever—
        do not abandon the works of your hands.

But the reason why we have not seen as much as us moving into the place of masteries is that we have to stop trying to make things happen acting like the world.
We have to win in the things we do in the Lord. But don't forget, to have a deeper life in Christ:

1. You must continue to strive in Christ to do so.
2. Timothy 2:1-5 says: Strive for a deeper life in Christ without being concerned so much about this world.
3. Strive for the Masteries because God will crown those who master the things He has called them to.

Now many of those things have not been done because of the things of the world seem to keep us so busy until we have not achieved the most important things we should have by now!

3. We can not achieve them alone; we need each other in order to experience the power which God has given to us (Luke 10:19).

In this world today only the strong will survive.

The word of God says be strong in the Lord and in the power of His might.

Luke 11:21 (New International Version)

[21] "When a strong man, fully armed, guards his own house, his possessions are safe.

Luke 11:22 (New International Version)

²² But when someone stronger attacks and overpowers him, he takes away the armor in which the man trusted and divides up the spoils."

Do you see what I see? Read that again: verse 22b says "he takes away the armor in which the man trusted." Understand this: the only way the stronger one can attack him and overpower him when he no longer have his armor.

We must learn how to use our armor and how to keep it useable. Some armor we are carrying around needs to be sharpened. When you don't use the armor it gets dull and stiff. We have to keep it sharp and lubricated with the oil of the Holy Spirit, praying in the Spirit.

The revelation of the power of God is so deep until it is hard to understand without praying in the Spirit. The power of God will stand up against anything that will try to attack you, especially if it comes into your house and tries to overtake you. That means whatever spirit comes into your house other than the Spirit of God as a child of God will be trespassing and violating your rights as a blood bought, Holy Spirit filled, born again, Children of God!!!

Romans 1:11 (New International Version)

^{11.} "I long to see you so that I may impart to you some spiritual gift to make you strong." Paul said how he longs to see you; meaning coming to where you are so that I may impart to you some spiritual gift to make you strong! Wow! What a powerful word. Paul said "I am power packed with power to give to you, enough to leave you with some spiritual gift, not just for you to speak in tongues and prophecy but to attack the stronger man who comes to steal from you!!!!!" Our stand is important to God. He said having done all to stand, stand and see the salvation of the Lord. Jesus said "No weapon formed against you shall prosper and every tongue that rise up against you in judgment is condemned"

Ephesians 6:10 (New International Version)

The Armor of God

^{10.} "Finally, be strong in the Lord and in his mighty power."
The armor of God was created for his children to combat the enemy and tear down the enemies' walls of defense that he tries to use against us.

This is how God wants the Church to go forth! He wants us to go with our armor intact and fully functioning, with no malfunctions operating. That is the reason why we have to be impacted with the strength of God through the power of the Holy Ghost, the gift God has given to us for power that cannot be reckoned with!

God Destroys Bondage

Bondage is one of the things God hates. Bondage is not healthy for those who are kept from giving all of their lives to God, all of their attributes to him as a glorious thank you to him! If someone does not love being in your company, allow them to go and live in Peace! When they are not allowing you the freedom God gave to you, then they are in some type of bondage. Don't hold a man against his will. In the church, I always say let whosoever will come. Not special people, but anybody who so desire and let the love of Jesus cover them and keep them in his presence.

Exodus 9:1-35 (New International Version) Check out what happens with those who try to hold us in bondage, who try to keep us from the will of our father, who desires us to worship Him!!

¹ Then the LORD said to Moses, "Go to Pharaoh and say to him, 'this is what the LORD, the God of the Hebrews, says: "Let my people go, so that they may worship me." ² If you refuse to let them go and continue to hold them back, ³ the hand of the LORD will bring a terrible plague on your livestock in the field—on your horses and donkeys and camels and on your cattle and sheep and goats. ⁴ But the LORD will make a distinction between the livestock of Israel and that of Egypt, so that no animal belonging to the Israelites will die.'"

⁵ The LORD set a time and said, "Tomorrow the LORD will do this in the land." ⁶ And the next day the LORD did it: All the livestock of the Egyptians died, but not one animal belonging to the Israelites died. 7 Pharaoh sent men to investigate and found that not even one of the animals of the Israelites had died. Yet his heart was unyielding and he would not let the people go.

The Plague of Boils

⁸ Then the LORD said to Moses and Aaron, "Take handfuls of soot from a furnace and have Moses toss it into the air in the presence of Pharaoh. ⁹ It will become fine dust over the whole land of Egypt, and festering boils will break out on men and animals throughout the land."

¹⁰ So they took soot from a furnace and stood before Pharaoh. Moses tossed it into the air, and festering boils broke out on men and animals. ¹¹ The magicians could not stand before Moses because of the boils that were on them and on all the Egyptians. ¹² but the LORD hardened Pharaoh's heart and he would not listen to Moses and Aaron, just as the LORD had said to Moses.

The Plague of Hail

¹³ Then the LORD said to Moses, "Get up early in the morning, confront Pharaoh and say to him, 'This is what the LORD, the God of the Hebrews, says: Let my people go, so that they may worship me, ¹⁴ or this time I will send the full force of my plagues against you and against your officials and your people, so you may know that there is no one like me in all the earth.

¹⁵ For by now I could have stretched out my hand and struck you and your people with a plague that would have wiped you off the earth. ¹⁶ But I have raised you up [a] for this very purpose, that I might show you my power and that my name might be proclaimed in all the earth. ¹⁷ You still set yourself against my people and will not let them go. ¹⁸ Therefore, at this time tomorrow I will send the worst hailstorm that has ever fallen on Egypt, from the day it was founded till now.

¹⁹ Give an order now to bring your livestock and everything you have in the field to a place of shelter, because the hail will fall on every man and animal that has not been brought in and is still out in the field, and they will die.'"

²⁰ Those officials of Pharaoh who feared the word of the LORD hurried to bring their slaves and their livestock inside. ²¹ But those who ignored the word of the LORD left their slaves and livestock in the field.

²² Then the LORD said to Moses, "Stretch out your hand toward the sky so that hail will fall all over Egypt—on men and animals and on everything growing in the fields of Egypt." ²³ When Moses stretched out his staff toward the sky, the LORD sent thunder and hail, and lightning flashed down to the ground. So the LORD rained hail on the land of Egypt;

²⁴ hails fell and lightning flashed back and forth. It was the worst storm in all the land of Egypt since it had become a nation. ²⁵ Throughout Egypt hail struck everything in the fields—both men and animals; it beat down everything growing in the fields and stripped every tree. ²⁶ The only place it did not hail was the land of Goshen, where the Israelites were.

²⁷ Then Pharaoh summoned Moses and Aaron. "This time I have sinned," he said to them. "The LORD is in the right, and I and my people are in the wrong. ²⁸ Pray to the LORD, for we have had enough thunder and hail. I will let you go; you don't have to stay any longer."

²⁹ Moses replied, "When I have gone out of the city, I will spread out my hands in prayer to the LORD. The thunder will stop and there will be no more hail, so you may know that the earth is the Lord's. ³⁰ But I know that you and your officials still do not fear the LORD God."

³¹ (The flax and barley were destroyed, since the barley had headed and the flax was in bloom. ³² the wheat and spelt, however, were not destroyed, because they ripen later.)

³³ Then Moses left Pharaoh and went out of the city. He spread out his hands toward the LORD; the thunder and hail stopped, and the rain no longer poured down on the land. ³⁴ When Pharaoh saw that the rain and hail and thunder had stopped, he sinned again: He and his officials hardened their hearts. ³⁵ So Pharaoh's heart was hard and he would not let the Israelites go, just as the LORD had said through Moses.

Exodus 10 (King James Version)

Many who are not serving God may have a spirit of bondage.

³ And Moses and Aaron came in unto Pharaoh, and said unto him, thus said the LORD God of the Hebrews, How long wilt thou refuse to humble thyself before me? Let my people go, that they may serve me.

After the Hail, the Locusts came to eat up everything else!

⁴ Else, if thou refuse to let my people go, behold, tomorrow will I bring the locusts into thy coast:

⁵ And they shall cover the face of the earth, that one cannot be able to see the earth: and they shall eat the residue of that which is escaped, which remain unto you from the hail, and shall eat every tree which grow for you out of the field:

Exodus 14 (New International Version)

¹ Then the LORD said to Moses, ² "Tell the Israelites to turn back and encamp near Pi Hahiroth, between Migdol and the sea. They are to encamp by the sea, directly opposite Baal

Zephon. [3] Pharaoh will think, 'The Israelites are wandering around the land in confusion, hemmed in by the desert.' [4] And I will harden Pharaoh's heart, and he will pursue them. But I will gain glory for myself through Pharaoh and all his army, and the Egyptians will know that I am the LORD." So the Israelites did this.

Fear is what keeps us in bondage; it takes Gods power to set us free from it!

[13] Moses answered the people, "Do not be afraid. Stand firm and you will see the deliverance the LORD will bring you today. The Egyptians you see today you will never see again. [14] The LORD will fight for you; you need only to be still."

Use the power of Faith God has given you, stretch forth your faith!

[15] Then the LORD said to Moses, "Why are you crying out to me? Tell the Israelites to move on. [16] Raise your staff and stretch out your hand over the sea to divide the water so that the Israelites can go through the sea on dry ground. [17] I will harden the hearts of the Egyptians so that they will go in after them. And I will gain glory through Pharaoh and all his army, through his chariots and his horsemen. [18] The Egyptians will know that I am the LORD when I gain glory through Pharaoh, his chariots and his horsemen."

[19] Then the angel of God, who had been traveling in front of Israel's army, withdrew and went behind them. The pillar of cloud also moved from in front and stood behind them, [20] coming between the armies of Egypt and Israel. Throughout the night the cloud brought darkness to the one side and light to the other side; so neither went near the other all night long.

God will use what he want to, just to get us free!

[21] Then Moses stretched out his hand over the sea, and all that night the LORD drove the sea back with a strong east wind and turned it into dry land. The waters were divided, [22] and the Israelites went through the sea on dry ground, with a wall of water on their right and on their left.

[23] The Egyptians pursued them, and all Pharaoh's horses and chariots and horsemen followed them into the sea. [24] During the last watch of the night the LORD looked down from the pillar of fire and cloud at the Egyptian army and threw it into confusion. [25] He jammed the wheels of their chariots so that they had difficulty driving. And the Egyptians said, "Let's get away from the Israelites! The LORD is fighting for them against Egypt."

[26] Then the LORD said to Moses, "Stretch out your hand over the sea so that the waters may flow back over the Egyptians and their chariots and horsemen." [27] Moses stretched out his

hand over the sea, and at daybreak the sea went back to its place. The Egyptians were fleeing toward it, and the LORD swept them into the sea. ²⁸ The water flowed back and covered the chariots and horsemen—the entire army of Pharaoh that had followed the Israelites into the sea. Not one of them survived.

²⁹ But the Israelites went through the sea on dry ground, with a wall of water on their right and on their left. ³⁰ That day the LORD saved Israel from the hands of the Egyptians, and Israel saw the Egyptians lying dead on the shore. ³¹ And when the Israelites saw the mighty hand of the LORD displayed against the Egyptians, the people feared the LORD and put their trust in him and in Moses his servant.

The word of God says that God desires that we prosper and be in health as our soul prosper (3John 2) our minds, will and emotion is involved in our stress, pain and bondages so God seek ways for us to get out of those things that keep us from serving Him freely. Bondages keep us away from God and give us a false way of worshiping God! Stay free from anything that does not allow you to serve God in its fullness. Don't get involved with others who do not serve God with their whole heart. Half heartiness gives place to other things that does not give God the glory that is due unto His name! Serve Him with your whole Heart and enjoy the Riches of His Glory!

Nehemiah 8:6; Revelation 7:11-12

Only the Strong survives!

"Don't worry! Be happy, what God promised he will bring it to pass?"
Remember this:

1. No Promise without Pursuit. What comes between promise and pursuit is patience and persistence! Daniel was persistent with what he was called to do because of the promise God had already spoken upon him; he did what he had to do. Even those with him vowed to only eat vegetables and drink water.

Daniel increased in knowledge, understanding and wisdom. He increased until he was the only one who had the gift of visions and dreams. The word says if you are faithful over a little he will make you ruler over much.

Daniel 2:48 (New International Version)

The story about Daniel shows us what commitment is to Gods will!

[48] Look at Daniel as he went through his trial! "Then the king placed Daniel in a high position and lavished many gifts on him. He made him ruler over the entire province of Babylon and placed him in charge of all its wise men."

2. No Vision without Purpose. What comes between vision and purpose is deception and power struggles! (Paul and Silas) they were locked in chains, on their hands and feet but they knew their purpose and Vision.

3. No Provision without a Position! What comes between provision and position is division! (The three Hebrew boys)

After they refused to bow and come out of the fiery furnace, they were promoted. They remained in a position as to say no, we will not bow to another God and their God will show up. Look what happened when they stood on God's word; They were promoted to a higher position.

Daniel 2:49 (New International Version)

[49] "Moreover, at Daniel's request the king appointed Shadrach, Meshach and Abednego administrators over the province of Babylon, while Daniel himself remained at the royal court."

4. No Promotion without a Plan! What comes between promotion and plan is pressure: Joseph had to resist to the point of fleeing from polisher's wife, he was under pressure! Much pressure but he was promoted through his pressure.

Genesis 39:1-23(New International Version)

Joseph and Polisher's Wife

[1] Now Joseph had been taken down to Egypt. Pasiphae, an Egyptian who was one of Pharaoh's officials, the captain of the guard, bought him from the Ishmaelites who had taken him there.

[2] The LORD was with Joseph and he prospered, and he lived in the house of his Egyptian master. [3] When his master saw that the LORD was with him and that the LORD gave him success in everything he did, [4] Joseph found favor in his eyes and became his attendant.

Potiphar put him in charge of his household and he entrusted to his care everything he owned. [5] From the time he put him in charge of his household and of all that he owned, the LORD blessed the household of the Egyptian because of Joseph.

The blessing of the LORD was on everything Potiphar had, both in the house and in the field. [6] So he left in Joseph's care everything he had; with Joseph in charge, he did not concern himself with anything except the food he ate.

Now Joseph was well-built and handsome, ⁷ and after a while his master's wife took notice of Joseph and said, "Come to bed with me!"

⁸ But he refused. "With me in charge," he told her, "my master does not concern himself with anything in the house; everything he owns he has entrusted to my care.

⁹ No one is greater in this house than I am. My master has withheld nothing from me except you, because you are his wife. How then could I do such a wicked thing and sin against God?" ¹⁰ And though she spoke to Joseph day after day, he refused to go to bed with her or even be with her.

¹¹ One day he went into the house to attend to his duties, and none of the household servants was inside. ¹² She caught him by his cloak and said, "Come to bed with me!" But he left his cloak in her hand and ran out of the house.

¹³ When she saw that he had left his cloak in her hand and had run out of the house, ¹⁴ she called her household servants. "Look," she said to them, "this Hebrew has been brought to us to make sport of us! He came in here to sleep with me, but I screamed. ¹⁵ When he heard me scream for help, he left his cloak beside me and ran out of the house."

¹⁶ She kept his cloak beside her until his master came home. ¹⁷ Then she told him this story: "That Hebrew slave you brought us came to me to make sport of me. ¹⁸ but as soon as I screamed for help; he left his cloak beside me and ran out of the house."

¹⁹ When his master heard the story his wife told him, saying, "This is how your slave treated me," he burned with anger. ²⁰ Joseph's master took him and put him in prison, the place where the king's prisoners were confined.

But while Joseph was there in the prison, ²¹ the LORD was with him; he showed him kindness and granted him favor in the eyes of the prison warden. ²² So the warden put Joseph in charge of all those held in the prison, and he was made responsible for all that was done there. ²³ The warden paid no attention to anything under Joseph's care, because the LORD was with Joseph and gave him success in whatever he did.

Genesis 41:42 (New International Version)

⁴² Then Pharaoh took his signet ring from his finger and put it on Joseph's finger. He dressed him in robes of fine linen and put a gold chain around his neck.

Genesis 41:44 (New International Version)

⁴⁴ Then Pharaoh said to Joseph, "I am Pharaoh, but without your word no one will lift hand or foot in all Egypt."

Now if we keep our eyes on the promises of God and His plans for our lives, we would not take such a long time to reach our destination. Because of so many interferences, we tend to stop looking unto Jesus and begin to search for other things to take us into the promise land which God has promised to give to us.

One of our main hindrances is doubt from others and defeat in our own eyes! We must handle this spirit of doubt and defeat from the spiritual side of the spectrum. If we try to handle it from the human side, the only thing we will accomplish is hard work without success! We have to deal with our spiritual understanding to change natural situations! The best thing we could ever do is get truly Born again and spirit filled! Change your limited thinking to ever increasing Wisdom!!!!

Our minds are not human minds when we become born again; we become more spiritual minded than human minded. At that point, we began to focus on what God said rather than what we see. What we see only gives us a temporary situation; we don't look at it as though it will be there tomorrow or forever. At anytime, things can change depending on what we say and what God said about it in His word. We also realize nothing is too hard for God to do.

Numbers 13: 17-25 (New International Version)

¹⁷ When Moses sent them to explore Canaan, he said, "Go up through the Negev and on into the hill country.

⁽¹⁸⁾ 1.   See what the land is like

2. and whether the people who live there are strong or weak, few or many.

(19) 3. What kind of land do they live in?

4.   Is it good or bad?

5.   What kind of towns do they live in?

6.   Are they unwilled or fortified?

²⁰⁾ 6. How is the soil? Is it fertile or poor?

7. Are there trees on it or not? Do your best to bring back some of the fruit of the land." (It was the season for the first ripe grapes.)

²³ When they reached the Valley of Eshkol, they cut off a branch bearing a single cluster of grapes. Two of them carried it on a pole between them, along with some pomegranates and figs. ²⁴ that place was called the Valley of Eshkol because of the cluster of grapes the Israelites cut off there. ²⁵ At the end of forty days they returned from exploring the land.

Report on the Exploration

Numbers 13: 26:—33

²⁶ They came back to Moses and Aaron and the whole Israelite community at Kadesh in the Desert of Paran. There they reported to them and to the whole assembly and showed them the fruit of the land. ²⁷ They gave Moses this account: "We went into the land to which you sent us, and it does flow with milk and honey! Here is its fruit. ²⁸ But the people who live there are powerful and the cities are fortified and very large. We even saw descendants of Anak there. ²⁹ The Amalekites live in the Negev; the Hittites, Jebusites and Amorites live in the hill country; and the Canaanites live near the sea and along the Jordan."

³⁰ Then Caleb silenced the people before Moses and said, "We should go up and take possession of the land, for we can certainly do it."

³¹ But the men who had gone up with him said, "We can't attack those people; they are stronger than we are." ³² And they spread among the Israelites a bad report about the land they had explored. They said, "The land we explored devours those living in it. All the people we saw there are of great size. ³³ We saw the Nephilim there (the descendants of Anak come from the Nephilim). We seemed like grasshoppers in our own eyes, and we looked the same to them."

Here are some things we need to stay in the race!

1. We must have a winning attitude
2. Trust when fear comes, don't faint!
3. Victory and determination no matter what we see!

Believe me that fear is always there between your victory and your promise.

First God gave us a promise: A land that flows with milk and honey!

Then, he said we must go and possess the land which he gave to us and our children which flows with milk and honey! God will never give us anything without giving us a way to process it.
Sometimes he will use our enemies to get it to us or give us favor but some way, somehow we will process it!
It's His promise and what he promised he will bring it to pass!

Today let's get rid of all of the things that have kept us from our promises! Some of us have allowed excuses to slow us down and stop depending on what God promised us, and not really moving forward into the assignment God gave us because of the fear factor. Be strong in the Lord and in the power of His might!

If you have not seen the promises of God fulfilled in your life like God's word promised, do understand there is nothing wrong with God's word. Rather, we need to increase our confidence in God's word because the word says all of his promises are ye and amen. All we should see in our heart is victory.

If you are low in faith and your victory level seems low, I dare you to take God's word as a sure thing today and receive the power of the Holy Ghost so you can go on to higher heights and deeper depths.

It's like being low on gas in your car. You know you can only go but so far with a certain amount of gas. So it is when your faith level is low and your determination is not where it should be, you can not move until you get a fill up. Today it's time for a fill upon the Holy Ghost. When you are low in fuel, you can't go too long without something to keep you going. Once you are filled, your faith will go so high that no body can tell you anything to discourage you about doing what God said you can do!

Stop allowing your situation to dictate to your flesh, telling you something is wrong and you will never succeed. No, it is how you are thinking and believing, what you are receiving in your heart about your self and your situation.

Stop gathering information that does not exist. Begin to depend on the Holy Spirit to get you where you need to go and get what you need!

A deeper Life series

Turn on your light!

If you are the light of the world your light should be turned on! Not off! You are the light of the world!

Matthew 5:14 (New International Version)

14 "You are the light of the world. A city on a hill cannot be hidden.

John 3:19 (New International Version)

19 This is the verdict: Light has come into the world, but men loved darkness instead of light because their deeds were evil.

John 9:5 (New International Version)

5 While I am in the world, I am the light of the world."

You are in the world but not of it!

John 8:12 (New International Version)

The Validity of Jesus' Testimony

12 When Jesus spoke again to the people, he said, "I am the light of the world. Whoever follows me will never walk in darkness, but will have the light of life."

The world loves its own! So if you are still in love with the world you are in love with something that is not in love with you! Satan is the God of this world and he makes men slaves to get what they want in this world without God Jehovah, the lover of our souls.

John 12:46 (New International Version)

[46] I have come into the world as a light, so that no one who believes in me should stay in darkness.

Matthew 16:26 (New International Version)

[26.] "What good will it is for a man if he gains the whole world, yet forfeits his soul? Or what can a man give in exchange for his soul?"

At the end when you see Jesus what will he say to you who live for him and are blessed by his hands?

Matthew 25:34 (New International Version)

[34] "Then the King will say to those on his right, 'Come, you who are blessed by my Father; take your inheritance, the kingdom prepared for you since the creation of the world.'"

Luke 16:11 (New International Version) [11] So if you have not been trustworthy in handling worldly wealth, who will trust you with true riches?"

Luke 16:10-13(The Message)

[10-13] Jesus went on to make these comments:
>If you're honest in small things,
>>you'll be honest in big things;
>if you're a crook in small things,
>>you'll be a crook in big things.
>If you are not honest in small jobs
>>who will put you in charge of the store?
>No worker can serve two bosses:
>>He'll either hate the first and love the second
>or adore the first and despise the second.
>>You can't serve both God and the Bank.

Luke 16:8-9 (The Message)

[8-9] "Now here's a surprise: The master praised the crooked manager and why? You may ask, because he knew how to look after himself. Streetwise people are smarter in this regard than law-abiding citizens. They are on constant alert, looking for angles, surviving by their wits. I want you to be smart in the same way—but for what is right—using

every adversity to stimulate you to creative survival, to concentrate your attention on the bare essentials, so you'll live, really live, and not complacently just get by on good behavior."

The world hates you! That is why when they see you changed and living different, they are player haters! They do things behind your back and smile in your face!
John 15:18-19 (The Message)

Hated by the World

18-19 "If you find the godless world is hating you, remember it got its start hating me. If you lived on the world's terms, the world would love you as one of its own. But since I picked you to live on God's terms and no longer on the world's terms, the world is going to hate you."

John 7:7 (New International Version)

7 "The world cannot hate you, but it hates me because I testify that what it does is evil."

Always remember this! For we wrestle not against flesh and blood but against principalities and powers and rules of this world.

2 Corinthians 10:3-6 (The Message)

3-6 The world is unprincipled. It's dog-eat-dog out there! The world doesn't fight fair. But we don't live or fight our battles the way the devil does—never have and never will. The tools of our trade aren't for marketing or manipulation, but they are for demolishing that entire massively corrupt culture.

We use our powerful God-tools for smashing warped philosophies, tearing down barriers erected against the truth of God, fitting every loose thought and emotion and impulse into the structure of life shaped by Christ. Our tools are ready at hand for clearing the ground of every obstruction and building lives of obedience into maturity."

Ephesians 6: 10-12 (The Message)

A Fight to the Finish

God is strong, and he wants you strong. So take everything the Master has set out for you, well-made weapons of the best materials. And put them to use so you will be able to stand up to everything the Devil throws your way. This is no afternoon athletic contest that we'll walk away from and forget about in a couple of hours. This is for keeps, a life-or-death fight to the finish against the Devil and all his angels."

I have to work while it is day because when night comes no man can work!
This is my Job

Titus 2:1-15 (The Message)

A God-Filled Life

1-6 "Your job is to speak out on the things that make for solid doctrine. Guide older men into lives of temperance, dignity, and wisdom, into healthy faith, love, and endurance. Guide older women into lives of reverence so they end up as neither gossips nor drunks, but models of goodness. By looking at them, the younger women will know how to love their husbands and children, be virtuous and pure, keep a good house, and be good wives. We don't want anyone looking down on God's Message because of their behavior. Also, guide the young men to live disciplined lives.

7-8 But mostly, show them all this by doing it yourself, incorruptible in your teaching, your words solid and sane. Then anyone who is dead set against us, when he finds nothing weird or misguided, might eventually come around.

9-10 Guide slaves into being loyal workers, a bonus to their masters—no back talk, no petty thievery. Then their good character will shine through their actions, adding luster to the teaching of our Savior God.

11-14 God's readiness to give and forgive is now public. Salvation's available for everyone! We're being shown how to turn our backs on a godless, indulgent life, and how to take on a God-filled, God-honoring life. This new life is starting right now, and is whetting our appetites for the glorious day when our great God and Savior, Jesus Christ, appears. He offered himself as a sacrifice to free us from a dark, rebellious life into this good, pure life, making us a people he can be proud of, energetic in goodness.

15 Tell them all this. Build up their courage, and discipline them if they get out of line. You're in charge. Don't let anyone put you down.

Renew your mind and move up to God standards of Life!

Romans 12:1-2 (The Message)

Place Your Life before God

¹⁻² "So here's what I want you to do, God helping you: Take your everyday, ordinary life—you're sleeping, eating, going-to-work, and walking-around life—and place it before God as an offering. Embracing what God does for you is the best thing you can do for him. Don't become so well-adjusted to your culture that you fit into it without even thinking. Instead, fix your attention on God. You'll be changed from the inside out. Readily recognize what he wants from you, and quickly respond to it. Unlike the culture around you, always dragging you down to its level of immaturity, God brings the best out of you, develops well-formed maturity in you."

(Ephesians 4:27) "Give no place to the devil, but resist the devil and he will flee!"

The devil goes around seeking whom he may devoir! Satan also goes about in various disguises.

Peter writes, (1 Peter 5:8). "Be sober, be vigilant, because your adversary the devil, as A ROARING LION, walked about, seeking whom he may devour; whom resist, steadfast in the faith"

Are you quite sure you must be a special exception, and that he will not "devour you, nor touch you?" If not, then "be sober," never be off guard one minute. Be watchful, for your adversary "walked about." He is your adversary as well as Christ's, and he goes about roaring as a lion, making a noise which deafens and frightens so many. The adversary "roars" by stirring up "flesh and blood." He as a spirit must find channels for his working. If he "roars" he must find a human voice to roar through.

Therefore the children of God should be on guard, and never act under the pressure of others, nor come to decisions in a time of storm. When there is clamor and strife of tongues, they should wait and be still. The adversary's "roar" is to drive them into a false step, and out of the calm, clear knowledge of the will of God.

Always recognize the adversary behind flesh and blood when there is clamor of voices, and stand still in the position of victory. When your eyes are opened to see and understand the devices of the enemy, you will lose sight of "flesh and blood," and realize that you must never act under the clamor of men. Alas, alas, the roaring lion can hide behind the greatest saint! Not with the saint's conscious co-operation, of course, but none the less true on that account.

This is one of the solemn things we have to learn today, as we discover how the enemy can use some of God's best children unconsciously to themselves, simply because they are not awake to his power and his devices.

The reason for this is that Satan works on the "natural" man. He makes the "natural man" come to you with his viewpoint (see Matt. 16: 22, 23), and his alarming pictures but you do not see the "roaring lion" in that; so you get frightened and wonder whether you are in the will of God; you get confused and lose your guidance, and the devil accomplishes his purpose.

Jesus has finished the work in those who were disciples. Now He is commissioning them to become leaders!

Relationships

Good homes, good Churches and good communities are built upon godly relationships.

The most common cause for failure in a relationship is a failure to live by and respond to God's Word, which results in the fullness of the Spirit.

When a believer is filled with the Spirit of God, he or she has the mind of God to go through relationship problems correctly.

There is a worldly way and a Godly way!

All relationships go through problem but they all can be resolved through the word of God. Christians should not use the pattern of this world to repair or fix their relationship, Christians <u>must</u> go to the word of God for answers. The answers God gives may not be what you want but they are what you need! One reason Christians don't go to the word of God for answers is because they have chosen the way that seems right but the way there is destruction!

If you are trying to fix the problem the way the world does it You are in for a big surprise!

The world says separate, divorce, shoot, kill, murder, but God's word says to love one another as Christ have loved you. While we were still a no-good sinner, God loved us.

Even when we did not want to have anything to do with God, He made a way for us, sending his only begotten Son to save us.

Eph. 4:30-5:18

When we are filled with the Spirit (not the same as baptized with the Spirit) we manifest the fruit of the Spirit as outlined in Galatians 5:22-24.

All interpersonal relationship problems stem from one or both parties walking in the flesh rather than walking in the Spirit.

In other words, if you are not in tune with the Spirit of God, you will not be in tune with others.

Look at Romans 12:1-2, 9-20; 13: 8-14.

There is something wrong with a person who continually has conflict with others and always has to make new friends because of relationship problems.

People of God, you should have some lasting friendships, and relationships! You will if you are saved and Spirit filled.

Here are a few simple thoughts on developing lasting Godly friendships and relationships:

1. Control your thoughts. Act 5:3 states about Ananias and Sapphire that "Satan hath filled their hearts to lie to the Holy Ghost . . ."
   2 Corinthians 10:3-6 tells us to cast down imaginations and bring our thoughts into captivity. When your thoughts are out of control, your life is out of control.

2. Control your tongue. (James 1:26; 3:1-18) A loose tongue will destroy a Godly relationship. In fact, it is Satan's greatest weapon. Colossians 4:6 says "Let your speech be always with grace seasoned with salt that you may know how ye ought to answer every man."

3. Control your temper. (Ephesians 4:30-32, 1 Peter 2:1-3) A loose temper is not excused by the Word of God. No Christian should brag on having a bad temper. That is like saying, "I am not under the control of the Holy Spirit." Also, it reveals that the person is walking in the flesh rather than the Spirit.

4. Don't lose sight of Satan's plan. (2 Corinthians 2:9-11) V.11 says "Lest Satan should get an advantage of us for we are not ignorant of his devices." (James 3:16) states "For where envying and strife is, there is confusion and every evil work." Love will always make a difference!

Read 1 Peter 3:7-17 and start working today to make and maintain lasting Godly relationships. Many times Satan wants to cripple your home, destroy your friendships and wants to testify about how he took advantage of your marriage, your relationship, or your friendship.

But thanks be to God who always causes us to triumph in life!

As a leader in Christ what is your position?

You are not placed in a position to tell everybody what to do but to show them what to do by the way you live and direct your business at home, on the Job, in your business, at Church and abroad!

Remember others are not just listening to what you say but they are watching what you do!! It only takes one person to see what you do to tell thousands what they saw you do!! You see God said flee from even the appearance of evil. Let me brake it down for you, if you are doing something that men may think is wrong most of the time it is because you are either in the wrong place or with the wrong people or persons.

There are three major things we must know as leaders: we must know that the three things that can get us out of the will of God are people, places and things; the people we hang with the things we do and the places we go! If I say I have changed and working in the kingdom to increase it, why would I be caught in a bar drinking with my old friend who I am trying to win to Christ? Then, you will try to tell them to come to your church with you. No, that is not what being in the position of a leader is! You are now guiding others into the right direction with how you govern your life.

As a leader in Christ you are someone others would follow! Not because of your name they are following you, but because of what they see you do and how you live. Others watch you to see if that is something they want to do before they begin to follow, so take this one thing in consideration before you say yes to God's will: Completely commit your whole heart to God and his purpose for your life that others may know Christ through your walk with him.

Luke 5:1-8 King James Version

One who is in a leadership position!

A Leader—A leader is someone who people follow (someone who guides or directs others), (somebody or something in lead); somebody in front of all others, a race or procession) (somebody in charge of others (the principal performer).
Leadership—the ability to guide, direct, or influence people!
Guidance—guidance or direction

Leaders—office or position of leader!
The office or position of the head of a political part or other body of people!
If you cannot be a good leader how can you lead others?
We can not say that we are leaders and are never at church when something going on where leaders are to lead.
For instance, if the leader who is over greeters is to make sure the guest are greeted with a nice welcome smile and a handshake when they enter the door does not show up but is doing something else somewhere else, would you call that a leader?
No, I can answer that for you! What is the use of having a leader over the greeters?
That person should want to make some improvements to their department. We must look at our approach to making our visitors feel at home when they come into the doors of the Church. How do we greet them? What do they see when they enter the door? How do they feel when they enter the door? At times, do we go out to help those who are parking and need assistance from one of our ushers which is our deacons at this time? Are we making our greeters improve in the way they look or the way they do things? Are they representing the kingdom like leaders? In every department we have to show God off not us.

In order for the Church to experience the deeper life, we must have people who are not just average people. We need leaders who are not just all about themselves. We need leaders who want to go to a higher dominion in their position.

God uses Ordinary people but they do extraordinary things, and because they do extraordinary things, extraordinary things happen from heaven above.

The number twelve comes in two meanings. It is derived from *Hebrews 4:12 for the word of God is living and active. Sharper than any double-edged sword, it penetrates even to dividing soul and spirit, joints and marrow; it judges the thoughts and attitudes of the heart.*

Disciples should make God's word come alive, and true by the way they live and judge their own thoughts and attitudes. We increase in knowledge and power. Disciples increase when we come together in one accord and in unity.

Look at How Jesus started out with Twelve disciples and ended up with 120 on the day of Pentecost (Acts 2:47) I ask that you read (Acts 2:1-21) to even get more of how our knowledge increase when we study Gods Word and how we increase in bringing others to a deeper life in Christ. Jesus poured into those who followed him and those who follow us will be poured into and will increase in knowledge.

Ordinary is just average and average people do average things. How many of you are tired of the average stuff happening in your life?

You know by now we should have conquered and overcame some things in our lives, but just ordinary will not take us to the extraordinary thing in life. I suggest you need to come on over to the deeper life.

Let go of your average thinking that is just getting the word and feeling you have enough. If you don't have the Holy Spirit ruling and reigning in your flesh, you will not tame the flesh to go beyond the ordinary.

Until we conquer the flesh in the Spirit, going into deeper things is limited. Why because the Holy Spirit will take you only as far as your flesh will allow you to go.

The truth will make you free but the flesh is rebellious as a mule and you have to put it under in the Spirit.

Show me someone out of line in the Spirit and I will show you a person who is going through the motion only.

They are not praying in the Spirit and not speaking the word over themselves and their family at all.

The Spirit of laziness comes upon those who are not drinking the wine of the Spirit every day. To see the extraordinary, we must reach out to God and let him know that we are not satisfied with just average anymore. It is time to move a little deeper out into the deep.

You have to do something to that flesh and that is inviting the wind of the Spirit into your life. He is called the Holy Spirit; the third person of the trinity fills you with power to move into the things God has prepared for you in your walk with God!!

A New Creature and His New Way of Life!

Ephesians 4:20-35 (King James Version)

(v. 20) But ye have not so learned Christ;

(v. 21) If **so be that ye have heard him, and have been taught by him, as the truth is in Jesus:**

1. **"Your Tools for living a new Life" (v.** 22) That ye put off concerning the former conversation the old man, which is corrupt according to the deceitful lusts;

<u>**"How to use**</u> "Strip yourselves of your former nature [put off and **discard** your old un-renewed self] which characterized your previous manner of life and becomes corrupt through lusts and desires that spring from delusion; **Let no corrupt communication proceed out of your mouth, but that which is good to the use of edifying, that it may minister grace unto the hearers. Those who knew you before and hear you now will immediately recognize that there has been a change in you because of your new conversation.**

2. **"Tool"** (23) and is renewed in the spirit of your mind;

<u>**"How to use"**</u>23And be constantly renewed in the spirit of your mind [having a fresh mental and spiritual attitude]; **allow your new attitude to express itself in a manner that will glorify God and the old will not get a chance to show up and keep you living in the old condemned unspiritual common attitude, but instead live in the new and wonderful, fresh and healthy one.**

Also, allow your new attitude to show up and make you and God look good and you will be rewarded from the Father for holding on to the new and doing away with the old condemned attitude. A fresh attitude is good to eat because it is fresh out of heavens' bakery, like fresh bread right out of the oven.

3. **"Tool"** 24And that ye put on the new man, which after God is created in righteousness and true holiness.

24. And put on the new nature (the regenerate self) created in God's image, [Godlike] in true righteousness and holiness. **You have a new tool now to use. Your new nature is just like Christ Jesus, when they crucified Him, He never said a word. Jesus depended on God to defend Him.**

The word says He will be your lawyer in the court room so, let others think what they want to. They are entitled to think the way they want to about you. You have to know the old you is dead. Don't let nothing and no one take your crown.

You can't see your crown, but the enemy knows you are a new creature. So he wants you to act like his kids still but he will be found to be in the wrong.

Every time you win in this fight, the angles give your crown a new shine Job. Blessings just keep on coming and men continue to be lead to Christ. Men will see your great work and glorify your Father which is in heaven.

4. **<u>"Tool"</u>** 25Wherefore putting away lying, speaks every man truth with his neighbor: for we are members one of another.

<u>How to use</u> 25 Therefore, rejecting all falsity and being done now with it, let everyone express the truth with his neighbor, for we are all parts of one body and members one of another. **The opportunity will always be available for you to lie because it will give you a chance to dig a deeper ditch for yourself to fall into. Therefore, outdo the devil by sticking to the truth and cause him to eventually fall into his own trap.**

5. **"Tool"** 26Be ye angry, and sin not: let not the sun goes down upon your wrath:

<u>How to use</u> 26When angry, do not sin; do not ever let your wrath (your exasperation, your fury or indignation) last until the sun goes down. **Don't hold on to what was done or said immediately, let it go because if you let it go, the other person will have to deal with it and you will set your own self free.**

6. **"Tool"** 27Neither give place to the devil.

How to use 27Leave no [such] room or foothold for the devil [give no opportunity to him]. **Don't leave the devil anything to eat off of that belongs to you. Make sure you take all the goods with you by cleaning up everything that he can find wrong in you. Quickly forgive and move on. Stop worrying about what someone did you; they will get their just reward and you will be able to stand back and watch it happen. If you don't give him anything, he will not have anything. Take your power with you by forgiving and moving on to your next time to rejoice. Rejoice in the Lord away and again I say rejoice.**

Mans limits and God's extremities!

Adam, we honor you as the fountainhead of our human race. What you became, we are. What you originally were, we would like to be. Permit us to analyze you in your garden. At first you were dirt shaped by divine fingers with head and body, with hands and feet, with heart and veins, with muscles and tissue, with digestive and nervous systems, but no soul, no life.

Then God breathed into your nostrils the breath of life and you became a living soul. Into your brain was placed a reasoning and a remembering mind; into your soul a felling conscience that advised, "Thou shall and thou shall not"; into your heart the tender emotions of love, joy, peace, and hope; and into your spirit life, ambition, zeal, and will.

Adam, you were the first and only created human being, the first and only one who bore the responsibility of keeping Eden and naming all animals, the first and only one from whose side a rib was taken from which was made a woman help meet, the first and only one to live in a complete state of innocence and fellowship with God, and the first and only one to be driven from the Garden of Eden lest you eat of the tree of life and live forever.

You were the first man, the first laborer, the first husband, the first father, the first sinner.

You were created by an act of God, consisting of body, soul, spirit, intellect.

You were responsible for the fall of human nature. The second Adam is responsible for redemption.

By honoring Adam we also take a look into our own lives and examine our position as God men and God women.

<u>Study</u> Genesis 1:26-28 Genesis 2, 3, 5; Romans 5:15-21 1Corinthians 15; Psalms 8:4-8

Now understand this: we are given all power, as God gave Jesus and Jesus gave it to us. That same power has been given unto us to choose what to do and what not to do. Some things are not accepted by God and some things are accepted by God. There are some limitations on us but not on God.

We must take the limits off of God and began to put limits on our flesh. Now remember in Christ there are no limits but in your flesh there are limits. Look at Adam; the only problem with him was he did not keep the garden. (Meaning to possess something or maintain something in your possession; to maintain somebody or something in a particular place or condition.)

Romans 5:12 (New International Version)

Death through Adam, Life through Christ

[12]Therefore, just as sin entered the world through one man, and death through sin, and in this way death came to all men, because all sinned—

    1 Timothy 2:14 (New International Version)

[14]And Adam was not the one deceived; it was the woman who was deceived and became a sinner.

Satan knew that he could not deceive Adam so he went to the woman and deceived him and that in it self brought condemnation upon Adam. Bringing condemnation upon all of us but Jesus with his unlimited power came and ejected the sin out of our lives and replaced it with the Love of God to restore us with the unlimited power to choose that which is right in the sight of God. So today we place limits on our flesh not to do what we always feel, but do what is right in the sight of God therefore taking the limits off of God and putting limits on our flesh. Put no confidence in the flesh.

Let's take a look at Cain; no doubt his conscience shouted to him, "don't do that, Cain!" But his envy argued, "Kill him, it's ok! You won't have any more trouble out of him again! Cain, overcome by his jealousy, met Abel in the field and killed him. They were the first two sons of Adam and Eve. Both of them were taught responsibility in the art of making a living. Cain was a farmer and Abel was a shepherd. Both of them communed with God and sought His approval. In order to gain His favor, both brought an offering.

Cain presented to God the fruit of the ground; Abel the tender ones of his flock. It is not clear, but the implication indicates that both boys had some knowledge as to what kind of offering would be acceptable to God. Abel respected God's will and offered the life of an animal with its blood and fat. Cain on the other hand dishonored God's will and made an offering, however, it did not meet God's requirements. Abel brought the firstlings of his flock. Cain, in process of time, made an offering.

That which was in Cain's heart led him to make a wrong offering led him also to resent God's rejecting it. His resentment turned to a hot jealous anger when he learned that God had accepted Abel and not his offering. Kill him, the spirit of jealousy shouted to Cain, and in the field Cain killed his brother Abel. What a disappointment to Adam! What a heart-braking situation to Eve! She could not understand why this happen to her two sons! God's judgment could not ignore such a crime, because Abel's blood cried out from the ground.

God's judgment upon him was severe, even more than Cain felt he could bear. Cain was now under the curse of God, banished from the face of God, exiled as a fugitive, and doomed as a fear-ridden vagabond. This lesson teaches us one thing about jealousness: it will come to anybody and entice them if they allow it to speak a word against another person who can even be your loved ones. Wherever there is a jealous spirit, anger is there also. The jealous spirit is not the dangerous spirit. It is anger that gives power to jealousness to cause it to kill, steal and destroy. (John 10:10) There is no limit to the destruction of jealousy once anger sets in. Most murders are committed because of the two spirits working together in mankind. Don't give place to the devil!

Cain had a chance to go and come back with a better sacrifice but jealousy would not allow him to say "I will not kill my brother" but I will go and get me a lamb and do what he is doing because both of them knew what the will of God was for the offering. But jealousy kept Cain from doing the same thing his brother was doing. God would have been happy to see the young brother copying what was right in his sight as an acceptable sacrifice.

Jealousy has a fear tactic with it: what if they do better than you? You are going to be made ashamed before everybody! That is what jealousy will say to you. Don't ever get to the place of envy that turns into jealousy and then anger then murder. But God has not given us the spirit of fear, but of power, love and a sound mind!

Somewhere as we become stronger saints, we must know God's order and how he wants the saints to operate in it! If we don't know how God's word is to be carried out, then we can not expect it to work for us correctly as God said in his word. This is a deeper life for the saints in Christ!!!

Prayer to Be Reckoned With

James 5:13-17 (The Message)

13-15 are you hurting? Pray. Do you feel great? Sing. Are you sick? <u>Call the church leaders together</u> to pray and anoint you with oil in the name of the Master. Believing-prayer will heal you, and Jesus will put you on your feet. And if you've sinned, you'll be forgiven—healed inside and out.

16-18 Make this your common practice: Confess your sins to each other and pray for each other so that you can live together whole and healed. The prayer of a person living right with God is something powerful to be reckoned with. Elijah, for instance, human just like us, prayed hard that it wouldn't rain, and it didn't—not a drop for three and a half years. Then he prayed that it would rain, and it did. The showers came and everything started growing again.

There are three types of people being addressed.

1. Those that are suffering or hurting. Praying and praying, and praying.
2. Those who are feeling great. Singing and praising God (dance, jumping, clapping, and making a joyful noise)
3. The word says those that are sick. Two kinds of healing will take place! Physical and spiritual healing is a part of the blessing from God almighty.

If you are hurting, you should be the main ones praying! If you are going through something or going through some suffering, not just the woman or not just the man needs to be praying. Both should be praying. Now I can understand why some don't want to pray because they don't see the need too! Simply that!

Do you feel great? Well you should be the loudest one here singing and dancing before the Lord. You have your victory just for feeling good! If you are not singing or dancing you need to be somewhere praying. Now don't get relaxed because you feel good! At some time, somewhere you need to be praying as well! Sometimes some of the saints need to be praying while the service is going on to destroy the yokes off of some of those who come hurting during the services!

Don't let that chair keep you bound to it, some of the leaders should be lead to remain in the office praying for the service from the time the services start until it finishes. Or take turns praying in the office or in the back! We need gap standers here! I asked God why so many leaders are sick and suffering he said "because they are not praying for others like they should be praying; they are so busy praying for themselves." That is one of the reasons it is taking them so long to see the overflow of blessings."

There are hang ups which need to be destroyed and old decade thoughts about others until they are not real in what they do and say! Old myths that they have heard of from long ago that they won't let go of. It is stealing from them and robbing them of the real joy I have given. Secret savers and they don't have the life savers. Because James is a man of faith, he has a passion for prayer. He dwells on the three areas of prayer.

1. When to pray
2. How to pray
3. And why pray (James 5:13-14)

James's first emphasis is on the diversity of circumstances for prayer. He wants the believers to put prayer into practice. One strong point James points out is to pray in all circumstances.

Look at the connection between 5:12 and 5:13; instead of fighting he is saying pray. Instead of walking in doubt and unbelief, Pray the word and watch what happens!

1. Pray in the time of trouble—this kind of trouble is not always suffering, it may be feeling like you are left out and something was not recognized.
2. Pray in times of happiness.

Is anyone cheerful or encouraged? Let me hear you say hallelujah!

You have to watch out because when we are happy, sometimes that may cause you to become complacent, and so we would pray less. But let me tell you—pray more. Now if you are happy, don't just sit and do nothing; pray and sing!!!!

When you are sick, we easily feel defeated. In times of sickness, weakness makes us feel hopeless, as if there were nothing to do. The biblical out look is the opposite:

there is something very significant to do, namely, to pray. Weakness is the very time for prayer. "Your helplessness is your best prayer" someone wrote. Pray in all kinds of circumstances. The habit of prayer should be, and indeed is, one of the most obvious features which differentiate a Christian from other people.

How to pray (James 5:14-16)

How prayer should operate in the church! Those meaning of the verses can be seen by isolating four practices which are pictured here or an effective prayer life . . .

We should call upon the elders of the church for prayer. The first fact is the sick persons call is an expression of their faith, which is one condition for effective prayer (James 5:16-17). The fact that the elders are the ones called is an expression of submission and unity in the church, which are additional conditions for powerful praying.

There is no indication of specialized spiritual gifts here. James envisions a spiritual power available to the church and exercised through the elders. Now this does not tell you to stop praying for yourself, but this is an order of the church. Bring the church into unity and oneness at the same time where there are relationships and binding love for one another. When the elders pray, it is to affirm the value of agreement by the church, for Jesus promised that agreement among Christians would unleash power for answered prayer (Matt. 18:19-20, John 15:7-17)

Pray in the name of the Lord. If the first practice expressed submission to each other in the church, this second practice expresses submission to the Lord himself. In this sense, it is not just a formula with which to pray, but a state in which to be praying: pray in union with Christ. (John 14:14,) (John 15:16) (Acts 16:23-24) James instructs us to anoint with oil. Not that the oil heals but it is something tangible that goes from one to another (Mark 6:13)

There are all kinds of prayer we need: prayers for the sick, healing, baptizing, casting out demons. (Luke 10:17) (Acts 2:28)

(Acts 3:6)(Acts9:34 and Acts 10:48)

Offer in faith (John 1:6): If you need faith, act in faith and you will receive it.
The effective prayer is praying united as repentant sinners: we should confess sins to each other and pray for each other. (James 5:15) When praying for the sick, if he has sinned, he will be forgiven. There is sometimes a connection between sin and illness;

It is possible, but not a necessity in every case. Physical illness, and the guilt may be interwoven, and the cure promises in (James 5:16)

When leaders pray for others, it builds faith-found relationships between them and God, which is where the power of the church lies. It stops us from attacking one another. Instead we pray for each others' healings. Instead of judging each other we help each other (James 4:12). Without praying for one another, our relationship suffers and the enemy gets place. James' assurance of results is the prayer will make the sick person well . . . . The lord will raise him up . . . . they will be forgiven . . . and they will be healed.

God makes much power available through its workings for those who will pray the prayer of Faith!

How very much can be accomplished through prayer of someone who is right with God.

You are the man in the mirror!

We look at ourselves every day. Well, let me state that a little differently. Most men look in the mirror every day and see themselves for who they are, but refuse to change because of the things they really enjoy that is not good for the sake of the gospel but for the sake of their own fleshly desires.

It is time for those of us who say we are the children of God to look at our lives in the mirror of the eye of God. The word of God says God knows our weakness and when we are weak, He is strong. Are we calling on our Father and turning our head away from the mirror when God begins to speak to us as we look and listen to his voice?

Sometimes I believe God's voice is ignored a lot these days. God is still speaking, my sisters and brothers, but are we listening? The word of God says let those who have ears hear what the spirit is saying. So, guess what? God is speaking, but we are ignoring his voice! Just ignore me and you will come to the understanding in a few trials. It is so funny how we can hear the voice of God for everybody else and refuse to hear for our selves. Please take heed and listen because things are getting more crucial every day in the lives of the people in this world.

A BIRD'S EYE VIEW

1 CORINTHIANS 2: 9

The power of the Holy Spirit gives us a bird's eye view of what God is doing in the earth.
You know if you look at what God is doing in the natural, you will not be encouraged to move on to greater things in the Lord.
Without the power of the Holy Spirit you cannot see what you need to see to encourage you to continue to go to higher heights and greater levels in the kingdom.
Without the help of the Holy Spirit, you are constantly fighting in the natural and that alone will wear you out. Through the Holy Spirit, you will have the power that will go beyond the natural, where the flesh cannot rule and reign over your life of wise decision making for the kingdom.
The bird's eye view is when you become an eagle. You fly high above the circumstances of life and soar through the clouds and the winds of life. When you become an eagle, your life is not predicated on what you can get from the earth to survive. It's what you get from God who has already prepared everything for you to survive from the heavenliest.

When you have a bird's eye view, you see things smaller than you, because you become larger and the earth below becomes smaller, but as long as you see the earth in the natural, the very things that look smaller when you are looking from a higher position will look greater than you when you are down where they are. God is calling us to a position where we can have a bird's eye view of what he has prepared for us.
This is where God is taking us. He is taking us to a place where eyes have not seen, ears have not heard, neither have it entered in the hearts of man the things he has prepared for those who Love him.

We must begin to see things from a bird's eye view perspective. If you want your words to be in the demonstration of the Spirit of God and the power of God-And not in the wisdom of man, you must allow the Holy Spirit to speak to your heart, speak through your eyes and see through your ears . . . Look at 1 Corinthians 2:7; those who crucified Jesus had no Idea that Jesus was the Savior of the World. Simply because they did not see, hear or had discernment.

They are the same today, People don't even recognize who they have before them because they have put all of God's people in a box and think we are all the same, one is no better than the other ones.
It's because they have seen so much unrighteousness in men and women who call themselves God's chosen ones.

We speak the wisdom of God in a mystery, even the hidden wisdom, which God ordained before the world unto our glory, which none of the princes of this world knew, for had they known it, they would not have crucified the Lord of glory. Men of old crucified the Lord so that we may live the life of blessing. These men hated the truth and righteousness until they tried to get rid of the way, the truth and the life, Jesus.

I want to give you this word we say to people every day and most of the time don't know what we are saying to them. It is a powerful word, Blessed means to be (Highly Favored of the Lord). If your eyes are constantly on the things of this world and you never give time to spiritual wisdom, you will not have spiritual discernment. Because in the spirit, you actually see with your ears and hear with your eyes and your heart is the judge of all things, naturally or spiritually.

Now please don't ask me how that works because I cannot lie to you and say I just do this or that.' But one thing I do know is there is a certain amount of reverence you have to have for the very presence of God's love and compassion for the things of the kingdom.

Discernment comes when you seek after God with all of your heart and lean not to your own understanding. (Prov. 2: 1-11). What I mean is—don't try to see everything in the natural and handle them from that standpoint. It will not happen. We must look at every situation in the eyes of God. (Matt.6: 33)(Prov. 3:5)

God calls us the greatest known bird and that is the eagle (Isaiah 40:31). Eagles fly high and are able to look directly into the storm and see beyond the storm. They fly toward the storm instead running from the storm. They live in the mountains, so everything that is below them are smaller and are seen with their keen eye. They are able to eat the fresh live fish from the sea because they can see the fish from the sky and go down to pluck them out of the water. When they become old and tired they go up into the mountain where there are waterfalls and bathe themselves.

They remain there and pluck out the old feathers and wait until they grow new feathers. They even rub their beak until they remove all of the old skin and wait until the new comes. They see themselves as new creatures; those who are in right standing and have renewed their strength.

Are you ready and willing to follow Jesus?

Matthew 16:24 If any man be willing to come after me—None is forced; but if any will be a Christian, it must be on these terms:

Let him deny himself, and take up his cross—A rule that can never be too much observed:

Let him in all things deny his own will, however pleasing, and do the will of God, even though it is painful.

Should we not consider all crosses, all things grievous to flesh and blood, as what they really are, as opportunities of embracing God's will at the expense of our own?

And consequently, as so many steps by which we may advance toward perfection?

We should make swift progress in the spiritual life, if we were faithful in this practice.

Crosses are so frequent, that whoever makes advantage of them, will soon be a great gainer.

Great crosses are occasions of great improvement; and the little ones, which come daily, and even hourly, make up in number what they want in weight.

We may in these daily and hourly crosses make effectual sacrifice of our will to God; which sacrifices, so often remembered and repeated, will soon amount to a great sum.

Let us remember then (what can never be sufficiently impressed) that God is the author of all events: that none is so small or inconsiderable, as to escape his notice and direction.

Every event therefore declares to us the will of God, to which, thus declared, we should heartily submit.

We should renounce our own to embrace it; we should approve and choose what his choice warrants as best for us.

Herein should we exercise ourselves continually; this should be our practice all the day long.

We should in humility accept the little crosses that are dispensed to us, as those that best suit our weakness.

Let us bear these little things, at least for God's sake, and prefer his will to our own in matters of so small importance.

And his goodness will accept these mean obligations for he despised not the day of small things. (Matt 10:38).

Be Strong and Courageous!!!

"Be strong and of a good courage; for unto this people shalt thou divide for an inheritance the land, which I swore unto their fathers to give them."—Joshua 1:6

This is not the time to faint and give up, says the Lord. This is the time to stand strong and be bold! The time has come for my children to throw off fear, weariness and weakness. This is the time to do greater works as I have told you in years past. Take off the spirit of heaviness and put on the garment of praise because your God has already made the way for you to enjoy the inheritance that he has promised to give you and your children.

The dictionary rendering of courage is bravery, boldness; and of the word strong, powerful. Be thou powerful and very brave is what the Lord meant.

The meaning of the word Courageous—The ability to face danger, difficulty, uncertainty, or pain without being overcome by fear or being deflected from a chosen course of action.

The meaning of the word Strong is—**emotionally resilient**—having the necessary emotional qualities to deal with stress, grief, loss, risk and other difficulties.

Say what you mean and mean what you say, stand and see the salvation of the Lord! Don't allow the enemy to bring fear upon you, you were bought with a price, you belong to God.

As the world looks at strength and courage, people go to great lengths to prove their skill and stamina in feats of strength and endurance—climbing great heights, crossing oceans alone and in a variety of different ways—but that is not what the Lord wants of his people.

Strength of mind and moral courage are the qualities to be acquired.

True, those who walked in faith before us endured hardness of a physical kind, and as we read the life of Joshua we recall the unpleasant task he had of smiting and subduing the surrounding nations before he could possess the land for the children of Israel. But it was a far deeper and more significant thing that was required of him.

As recorded in the last few verses of Joshua Chapter One, the children of Israel were willing to accept him if he would keep faith with God and give them good leadership.

There are many people who lived to leave us an example of how we should live today. Look at Job! We recall the very severe trial that Job had to endure. Wracked with pain, and passing through a time of mental anguish, he was forced to listen to the arguments of worldly-wise men. His resistance to obeying the voice of his wife "curse God and die," and his confidence in God in saying, "If he slay me, yet will I trust him." It proved that although he was unable to combat their arguments, his faith was still strong.

The whole book of Job revealed the fortitude of this man of God, showing a picture of the suffering of the whole world of mankind and their final deliverance and inheritance.

Now let us look at Gideon. Recall his strength of endurance and courage, and his great trust and faith in God when the numbers were narrowed down to three hundred. In Judges Chapter 7, we have a wonderful picture of the way in which God's ordained order took place and those who would assist Gideon in the remarkable victory that was his.

The simple test of how they drank the waters had such an effect on them being prepared for any emergency. It makes a difference today how we fight in faith. We take so much for granted. It's time for us to refresh our minds as to the way God dealt with his servant and how he is still doing it today!

We read of the highest point of their victory, how they took up strategic places (one hundred on each of three sides of the Midianites), how they had lamps in their pitchers, and trumpets in their hands, and at a command from Gideon they "brake the pitchers and holding the lamps in their left hands and the trumpets in their right hands to blow as one: they cried, The sword of the Lord, and of Gideon.

And they stood every man in his place round about the camp: and all of the host ran, and cried, and fled."—Judges 7:20, 21.

How do these reflections affect us? Are we being strong and very courageous in our present, everyday experiences? Do we trust sufficiently? Are we bold to come to the throne of heavenly grace to get the necessary strength to assist us in our trials and difficulties?

Again, let us think for a moment how we react in times of national and international stress. These upheavals sometimes make us fearful, and as human beings we shrink from them, but should we not rather look on them as additional opportunities to prove ourselves?
We are instructed to be more than conquers (overcomes); if this is to be true of us, we need to be equipped with the whole armor of God. We need to be sure that it is securely buckled on us, that it is kept bright and shining, and that there are no cracks anywhere, and particularly, we should keep our eyes ever on the goal set before us, to the end that we shall be bold and courageous (overcomes) through Jesus Christ our Lord.

Now, the great God of the universe has called us to be joint-heirs with his son Jesus Christ. Just as he dealt with the heroes of faith, whose lives we have briefly touched on foregoing; He dealt with them by fighting their battles, preparing the way for them, cheering, encouraging, and fortifying them when they lost hope; so does He dealt with us if we are willing and obedient.

If we are truly His, and his spirit witness with our spirit that we are the sons of God, then each of us can claim the promise: the Quickness of abilities to discern what is and what is not is within us to chose to walk in total awareness that he is with us. His promise is that He will never leave us nor forsake us. He said you would not have to fight in this fight, just stand be strong and courageous and see the salvation of the Lord. Only through the eye of faith are we able to remain steadfast, unmovable always abounding in his love. Be still and know that I am God; I will be exalted in the earth." Said the Lord! (Ps. 46:9, 10)

Psalm 46:9-10 (Contemporary English Version)

⁹God brings wars to an end
>All over the world
>He breaks the arrows,
>Shatters the spears,
>And burns the shields
¹⁰Our God says, "Calm down,
>and learn that I am God!
>All nations on earth
>will honor me."

Psalm 46:8-10 (The Message)

[8-10] Attention, all! See the marvels of GOD!
    He plants flowers and trees all over the earth,
Bans war from pole to pole,
    breaks all the weapons across his knee.
"Step out of the traffic! Take a long,
    loving look at me, your High God,
above politics, above everything

AN ATTITUDE OF GRATITUDE

Luke 17 (New International Version)
Luke 17:1-19

Sin, Faith, Duty

[1] Jesus said to his disciples: "Things that cause people to sin are bound to come, but woe to that person through whom they come. [2]It would be better for him to be thrown into the sea with a millstone tied around his neck than for him to cause one of these little ones to sin. [3]So watch yourselves.

   "If your brother sins, rebuke him, and if he repents, forgive him. [4]If he sins against you seven times in a day, and seven times comes back to you and says, 'I repent,' forgive him."
[5]The apostles said to the Lord, "Increase our faith!"
[6]He replied, "If you have faith as small as a mustard seed, you can say to this mulberry tree, 'Be uprooted and planted in the sea,' and it will obey you.
[7] "Suppose one of you had a servant plowing or looking after the sheep. Would he say to the servant when he comes in from the field, 'Come along now and sit down to eat'? [8]Would he not rather say, 'Prepare my supper, get yourself ready and wait on me while I eat and drink; after that you may eat and drink'? [9]Would he thank the servant because he did what he was told to do? [10]So you also, when you have done everything you were told to do, should say, 'We are unworthy servants; we have only done our duty.'"

Ten Healed of Leprosy

[11]Now on his way to Jerusalem, Jesus traveled along the border between Samaria and Galilee.
[12]As he was going into a village, ten men who had leprosy[a] met him. They stood at a distance
[13]and called out in a loud voice, "Jesus, Master, have pity on us!"

¹⁴ When he saw them, he said, "Go, and show yourselves to the priests." And as they went, they were cleansed.

¹⁵ One of them, when he saw he was healed, came back, praising God in a loud voice. ¹⁶He threw himself at Jesus' feet and thanked him—and he was a Samaritan.

¹⁷Jesus asked, "Were not all ten cleansed? Where are the other nine? ¹⁸Was no one found to return and give praise to God except this foreigner?" ¹⁹Then he said to him, "Rise and go; your faith has made you well."

Ezra 3 (New International Version)
Ezra 3:10-13

Rebuilding the Altar

¹⁰ When the builders laid the foundation of the temple of the LORD, the priests in their vestments and with trumpets, and the Levites (the sons of Asaph) with cymbals, took their places to praise the LORD, as prescribed by David king of Israel. ¹¹ With praise and thanksgiving they sang to the LORD:

> "He is good;
> his love to Israel endures forever."

And all the people gave a great shout of praise to the LORD, because the foundation of the house of the LORD was laid. ¹² But many of the older priests and Levites and family heads, who had seen the former temple, wept aloud when they saw the foundation of this temple being laid, while many others shouted for joy. ¹³ No one could distinguish the sound of the shouts of joy from the sound of weeping, because the people made so much noise. And the sound was heard far away.

Now the older priests and Levites and their family heads was still stuck back in the yesterdays, when the old temple was built by Solomon. They was so sad until their attitudes took them to a place of sorrow instead of rejoicing they had a bad attitude toward the new temple. Get out of lodibar and come on over to Bethel where there is a time of gratitude a time of thanksgiving.

Genesis 35 (New International Version)
Genesis 35: 1-13

Jacob Returns to Bethel

¹ Then God said to Jacob, "Go up to Bethel and settle there, and build an altar there to God, who appeared to you when you were fleeing from your brother Esau." In other words

go back to the place I blessed you and thank me for what I did for you even though you did wrong and should have been died by now, go back and give thanks with a new attitude of forgiveness! Your life should have been taken away from you because of the things you did to your brother but go back and show your gratitude toward me for keeping you Jacob.

² So Jacob said to his household and to all who were with him, "Get rid of the foreign gods you have with you, and purify yourselves and change your clothes. ³ Then come, let us go up to Bethel, where I will build an altar to God, who answered me in the day of my distress and who has been with me wherever I have gone." ⁴ So they gave Jacob all the foreign gods they had and the rings in their ears, and Jacob buried them under the oak at Shechem. ⁵ Then they set out, and the terror of God fell upon the towns all around them so that no one pursued them.

⁶ Jacob and all the people with him came to Luz (that is, Bethel) in the land of Canaan.

⁷ There he built an altar, and he called the place El Bethel, because it was there that God revealed himself to him when he was fleeing from his brother.

⁸ Now Deborah, Rebekah's nurse, died and was buried under the oak below Bethel. So it was named Allon Bacuth.

⁹ After Jacob returned from Paddan Aram (**Paddan** Aram or Padan-aram was an early Aramean kingdom in Mesopotamia). God appeared to him again and blessed him. ¹⁰ God said to him, "Your name is Jacob, but you will no longer be called Jacob; your name will be Israel." So he named him Israel.

¹¹ And God said to him, "I am God Almighty be fruitful and increase in number. A nation and a community of nations will come from you, and kings will come from your body. ¹² The land I gave to Abraham and Isaac I also give to you, and I will give this land to your descendants after you." ¹³ Then God went up from him at the place where he had talked with him.

God wants to reveal himself to you and your children if you would change your attitude and gratitude of thanksgiving. Thank God for what he has done and thank him for what he is doing right now! Stay out of the old trash of life we have had enough of that let's make a joyful noise for the great things God is doing right now. This is the day that the Lord has made as well as yesterday but yesterday is gone and this Is a new day with brand new happenings going on can't you feel it? Can you hear it?

1 Kings 18:36-45 (New International Version)

³⁶ At the time of sacrifice, the prophet Elijah stepped forward and prayed: "O LORD, God of Abraham, Isaac and Israel, let it be known today that you are God in Israel and that I am your servant and have done all these things at your command. ³⁷ Answer me, O LORD; answer me, so these people will know that you, O LORD, are God, and that you are turning their hearts back again."

³⁸ Then the fire of the LORD fell and burned up the sacrifice, the wood, the stones and the soil, and also licked up the water in the trench.

³⁹ When all the people saw this, they fell prostrate and cried, "The LORD—he is God! The LORD—he is God!"

⁴⁰ Then Elijah commanded them, "Seize the prophets of Baal. Don't let anyone get away!" They seized them, and Elijah had them brought down to the Kishon Valley and slaughtered there.

⁴¹ And Elijah said to Ahab, "Go, eat and drink, for there is the sound of a heavy rain." ⁴² So Ahab went off to eat and drink, but Elijah climbed to the top of Carmel, bent down to the ground and put his face between his knees.

⁴³ "Go and look toward the sea," he told his servant. And he went up and looked.

"There is nothing there," he said.
Seven times Elijah said, "Go back."

⁴⁴ The seventh time the servant reported, "A cloud as small as a man's hand is rising from the sea."

So Elijah said, "Go and tell Ahab, 'Hitch up your chariot and go down before the rain stops you.'"

⁴⁵ Meanwhile, the sky grew black with clouds, the wind rose, a heavy rain came on and Ahab rode off to Jezreel. ⁴⁶ The power of the LORD came upon Elijah and, tucking his cloak into his belt, he ran ahead of Ahab all the way to Jezreel.

Be grateful for all the things God has given to you and brought you out of with a high hand!

CAN YOU SEE THE KINGDOM OF GOD?

NOW MANY OF YOU MAY BE ASKING YOUR SELF, HOW CAN
I SEE THE KINGDOM.OF GOD? WELL, I AM GLAD YOU ASKED
BUT FIRST I NEED TO EXPLAIN SOMETHING TO YOU ABOUT THE KINGDOM
OF GOD. IS THAT OK?

NOW, LET ME TELL YOU WHAT THE KINGDOM IS NOT.

- THE KINGDOM OF GOD IS NOT OF MEAT AND DRINK AND OUTWARD
  RELIGION (**ROMANS 14:17-18**)
- THE KINGDOM OF GOD IS NOT IN WORD BUT IN POWER
- **(1CORINTHIANS 4:20)**

BUT THIS IS WHAT IT IS! IT IS RIGHTEOUSNESS, PEACE, AND JOY IN THE
HOLY GHOST.

(**LIFE APPLICATION**) THE KINGDOM OF GOD IS NOT A MATTER OF WHAT
WE EAT OR DRINK, BUT OF LIVING A LIFE OF GOODNESS AND PEACE AND
JOY IN THE HOLY SPIRIT.

IF YOU SERVE GOD WITH THIS ATTITUDE, YOU WILL PLEASE GOD.

AND OTHER PEOPLE WILL APPROVE YOU TOO. SO LET US AIM FOR HARMONY
IN THE CHURCH AND STRIVE TO BUILD EACH OTHER UP.

THE WORD OF GOD SAYS IN (**JOHN 3:3**) EXCEPT A MAN BE BORN AGAIN HE CAN NOT SEE THE KINGDOM. NOW, LOOK AT

(**JOHN 3: 5**) EXCEPT A MAN BE BORN OF THE WATER (NATURAL BIRTH) AND THE SPIRIT (ACCORDING TO THE WORD OF GOD) HE CAN NOT ENTER THE KINGDOM. AS THE NATURAL MAN HEARS THE WIND, SO THE MAN BORN AGAIN HEARS THE VOICE OF THE SPIRIT.

IN CONCLUSION, KINGDOM IS WITHIN YOU! LOOK AT (**LUKE 17:20-21**) MEANING YOU ARE FILLED WITH THE SPIRIT OF GOD

I BELIEVE THAT WE AS BORN AGAIN CHILDERN OF GOD NEED TO SEEK THE KINGDOM MORE AND MORE WITHIN US. (MATTHEWS 6:33) SEEK YE FIRST THE KINGDOM OF GOD AND HIS RIGHTEOUSNESS AND ALL OF THESE THINGS WILL BE ADDED UNTO YOU.

I BELIEVE IT IS TIME TO EXAMINE YOURSELF TO SEE WHETHER YOU ARE IN THE FAITH: (**2CORINTHIANS 13:5**) PROVE YOUR OWN SELVES, HOW THAT JESUS CHRIST IS IN YOU, EXCEPT YE BE REPROBATES?

The word says in (**JOHN 14:16-17**) THE SPIRIT OF TRUTH, WHOM THE WORLD CANNOT RECEIVE BECAUSE IT SEETH HIM, NOT, NEITHER KNOWETH HIM: BUT YE KNOW HIM; FOR HE DWELLETH WITH YOU, AND SHALL BE IN YOU.

LUKE 11: 9-13 THE KINGDOM IS HERE AND WANTS TO LIVE IN YOU RICHLY. WE ARE EARTHEN VESSELS WITH HEAVENLY TREASURES.

MANY DON'T GET ALL THAT GOD HAS PROMISED THEM BECAUSE THEY DON'T KEEP THE FAITH AND THEY LOSE OUT OF THE GREATEST PROMISES HEAVEN HAS TO OFFER THEM.

You must be prepared for purpose in your life. It will not wait on you; you have to wait on it. But, once it comes into your life, you cannot just guess you will take on this challenge. Your steps have been ordered and righteousness goes before you and prepares the way.

Psalm 85:12-13 (New International Version)

¹² The LORD will indeed give what is good,
     and our land will yield its harvest.

¹³ Righteousness goes before him
and prepares the way for his steps.

Now many of us continue to ask God what is my purpose? Understand this Most of the time your purpose lies in your problems.

Whenever you have a problem with money it is your purpose in life to find the money and make it happen where you are having the greatest problem. Sometimes it is necessary for you to go through some things in the area God will use you to be a blessing in your life time. You will have more than enough if your focus is on how you can help others get money! Help them by finding ways to remove obstacles out of others way and before you know it money will begin to overtake you!

Isaiah 57:14 (New International Version)

Comfort for the Contrite

¹⁴ And it will be said:
"Build up, build up, and prepare the road!
Remove the obstacles out of the way of my people."

Mark 1:2 (New International Version)

²It is written in Isaiah the prophet:
"I will send my messenger ahead of you,
who will prepare your way"

There is a message in your misery. There is a revelation in our revolution. Nothing just happens when you are a child of God. God makes ways to prosper you!
Psalms 1: 1-3

Look, if the job you believe for doesn't show up, then you needs to show up with a job. Somebody is going through the same thing you are going through and you are the only one who has been given the power to make it happen.

Sometimes God is setting you up to do something you should have done years ago, but never saw the need to do it. Meaning you need to see where God wants you to start making jobs for others.

Inside of you is a company, so why don't you get started with it now, because God wants to finance it supernaturally. This is the best time to go for it; you have nothing to lose.

Start it at home in your house where you have no expense at all other than what you have to believe God for already. Your rent will be paid and the other things you have to believe for anyway.

One thing came to mind when I thought about some things you can do. It won't cost you anything but will cost others something.

One is typing résumés for people who need jobs and need a professionally designed résumé. Place an ad in the paper and name it (**Rejoicing Resume' & Company).**

When you begin to understand purpose and you reach to receive what God has for you "This is what your ad may want to say! "We are here for you! Just one call away, get your Job today with the best ever Resume' Call—@ 999-888-0000) our Resumes with you in Mind. Professional and precisely designed with you in mind, call today and get your desired position, call me Betty and make your dream come true call 225-000-9999.

(**The New FitForLife Company U.S.A.**). If you are tired of the old you, become brand new with The New You (FitForLife Company USA). If you are tired of looking at yourself, why would you think someone else wants to look at you? Come and find the new you today.

Here's another company you can start. Set up a counseling service for single women and men who are going through self esteem syndrome conditions. (Set up a Job Seekers Company for security positions in the malls all over (Your City)

If you don't have the man or woman in your life that you believe you need, then you need to be the one who will set up a place for singles to have a chance to meet new singles like you. Be a problem solver for yourself and for others.

Go to places of business that's hurting right now and drum up some business with your ideas and let them know that you have an idea which will work for any business who will give it a try. Give them a price for your ideal.
Like this for instance: Singles night ages 17 to 95 Meet and Greet and it will only cost a measly $60.00. And for every $60.00, you get half. Put together an activity that will draw singles to that place. You know what they are looking for, so do it. Make it happen!!!! Don't be afraid, just do it!!!!
Have something for out of towners coming in just for the affair. Book a hotel and make it a business for yourself during the football seasons.

Stop looking for people to make a position for you. You make the job and the position for yourself and others just like you. Just do it because your daddy says it's ok!

Whatever u are lacking for in this life you need to begin to supply it for someone else and watch what God will do for you in the mist of the trial. Yes, I said trial because anything you do for the Lord or in the name of the Lord, you will experience trials. Trials don't move me anymore because I am just like Paul when he said I know how to be a base and I know how to be abounded.

The word says God will supply all of our needs according to his riches in Glory. (Phil. 4:19).
Now, I begin to ask God about his riches in Glory and it is different from his riches in heaven but he said in Glory.

Now if you look up the word Glory it means the very presence of God. Meaning wherever God's presence is, his Glory is there and if His glory is there His riches are there too.

Exodus 15:11 (New International Version)

¹¹ "Who among the gods is like you, O LORD?
    Who is like you—
    majestic in holiness,
    awesome in glory,
    working wonders?

Now that we know that God's riches show up in his Glory, what makes God's presence available to us as children of God? Well I can understand that Faith brings God's presences in the midst of us. So whenever there is fear, worry, double mindedness, sadness and weariness, God's presence will not be in the midst of us.
He is a very present Help in the time of need! (Psalms 46:1)

Now why do we need God's presence? We need his very presence because he always come to present us with the things we have not seen, we have not heard, and even have not entered in our heart the things he has for us. So, he brings those things to us when we get in one accord and become united as one in the spirit. That is why I keep ministering about the importance of us being in one accord and in unity.

God is not the author of confusion but of wholeness and oneness. One will put 1,000 demons to flight but two will put ten thousand demons to flight, so if two will put 10,000 to flight, that means when two come together we are nine thousand more stronger than the 1,000 demons.

Deuteronomy 8 (New International Version)

Do Not Forget the LORD

[1] Be careful to follow every command I am giving you today, so that you may live and increase and may enter and possess the land that the LORD promised on oath to your forefathers. [2] Remember how the LORD your God led you all the way in the desert these forty years; to humble you and to test you in order to know what was in your heart, whether or not you would keep his commands. [3] He humbled you, causing you to hunger and then feeding you with manna, which neither you nor your fathers had known, to teach you that man does not live on bread alone but on every word that comes from the mouth of the LORD. [4] Your clothes did not wear out and your feet did not swell during these forty years. [5] Know then in your heart that as a man disciplines his son, so the LORD your God disciplines you. [6] Observe the commands of the LORD your God, walking in his ways and revering him. [7] For the LORD your God is bringing you into a good land—a land with streams and pools of water, with springs flowing in the valleys and hills; [8] a land with wheat and barley, vines and fig trees, pomegranates, olive oil and honey; [9] a land where bread will not be scarce and you will lack nothing; a land where the rocks are iron and you can dig copper out of the hills.

[10] When you have eaten and are satisfied, praise the LORD your God for the good land he has given you. [11] Be careful that you do not forget the LORD your God, failing to observe his commands, his laws and his decrees that I am giving you this day. [12] Otherwise, when you eat and are satisfied, when you build fine houses and settle down, [13] and when your herds and flocks grow large and your silver and gold increase and all you have is multiplied, [14] then your heart will become proud and you will forget the LORD your God, who brought you out of Egypt, out of the land of slavery.

[15] He led you through the vast and dreadful desert, that thirsty and waterless land, with its venomous snakes and scorpions. He brought you water out of hard rock. [16] He gave you manna to eat in the desert, something your fathers had never known, to humble and to test you so that in the end it might go well with you. [17] You may say to yourself, "My power and the strength of my hands have produced this wealth for me." [18] But remember the LORD your God, for it is he who gives you the ability to produce wealth, and so confirms his covenant, which he swore to your forefathers, as it is today.

[19] If you ever forget the LORD your God and follow other gods and worship and bow down to them, I testify against you today that you will surely be destroyed. [20] Like the nations

the LORD destroyed before you, so you will be destroyed for not obeying the LORD your God.

Ezekiel 37 (New International Version)

Ezekiel 37

The Valley of Dry Bones

¹ The hand of the LORD was upon me, and he brought me out by the Spirit of the LORD and set me in the middle of a valley; it was full of bones. ² He led me back and forth among them, and I saw a great many bones on the floor of the valley, bones that were very dry. ³ He asked me, "Son of man, can these bones live?"

I said, "O Sovereign LORD, you alone know."

⁴ Then he said to me, "Prophesy to these bones and say to them, 'Dry bones, hear the word of the LORD! ⁵ This is what the Sovereign LORD says to these bones: I will make breath [a] enter you, and you will come to life. ⁶ I will attach tendons to you and make flesh come upon you and cover you with skin; I will put breath in you, and you will come to life. Then you will know that I am the LORD.'"

⁷ So I prophesied as I was commanded. And as I was prophesying, there was a noise, a rattling sound, and the bones came together, bone to bone. ⁸ I looked, and tendons and flesh appeared on them and skin covered them, but there was no breath in them.

⁹ Then he said to me, "Prophesy to the breath; prophesy, son of man, and say to it, 'this is what the Sovereign LORD says: Come from the four winds, O breath, and breathe into these slain, that they may live.' "10 So I prophesied as he commanded me, and breath entered them; they came to life and stood up on their feet—a vast army.

¹¹ Then he said to me: "Son of man, these bones is the whole house of Israel. They say, 'Our bones are dried up and our hope is gone; we are cut off.' ¹² Therefore prophesy and say to them: 'this is what the Sovereign LORD says: O my people, I am going to open your graves and bring you up from them; I will bring you back to the land of Israel. ¹³ Then you, my people, will know that I am the LORD, when I open your graves and bring you up from them. ¹⁴ I will put my Spirit in you and you will live, and I will settle you in your own land. Then you will know that I the LORD have spoken, and I have done it, declares the LORD.'"

One Nation under One King

¹⁵ The word of the LORD came to me: ¹⁶ "Son of man, take a stick of wood and write on it, 'Belonging to Judah and the Israelites associated with him.' Then take another stick of wood, and write on it, 'Ephraim's stick, belonging to Joseph and all the house of Israel associated with him.' ¹⁷ Join them together into one stick so that they will become one in your hand.

¹⁸ "When your countrymen ask you, 'Won't you tell us what you mean by this?' ¹⁹ say to them, 'This is what the Sovereign LORD says: I am going to take the stick of Joseph—which is in Ephraim's hand—and of the Israelite tribes associated with him, and join it to Judah's stick, making them a single stick of wood, and they will become one in my hand.' ²⁰ Hold before their eyes the sticks you have written on ²¹ and say to them, 'this is what the Sovereign LORD says: I will take the Israelites out of the nations where they have gone.

I will gather them from all around and bring them back into their own land. ²² I will make them one nation in the land, on the mountains of Israel. There will be one king over all of them and they will never again be two nations or be divided into two kingdoms. ²³ They will no longer defile themselves with their idols and vile images or with any of their offenses, for I will save them from all their sinful backsliding, [b] and I will cleanse them. They will be my people, and I will be their God.

²⁴ "'My servant David will be king over them, and they will all have one shepherd. They will follow my laws and be careful to keep my decrees. ²⁵ They will live in the land I gave to my servant Jacob, the land where your fathers lived. They and their children and their children's children will live there forever, and David my servant will be their prince forever. ²⁶ I will make a covenant of peace with them; it will be an everlasting covenant.

I will establish them and increase their numbers, and I will put my sanctuary among them forever. ²⁷ My dwelling place will be with them; I will be their God, and they will be my people. ²⁸ Then the nations will know that I the LORD make Israel holy, when my sanctuary is among them forever.'"

AN EXCELLENT SPIRIT WAS FOUND IN HIM

"... They could find none occasion nor fault; forasmuch as he was faithful, neither was there any error or fault found in him." Daniel 6:4

The presidents and princes sought to snare Daniel's life because he was preferred by the King. He was preferred not because of his great deeds, but because of his excellent spirit. They were seeking to trap Daniel! They began to search for anything they could bring occasion against him but found he was blameless in his life. They brought a decree before the king only as a means to snare Daniel.

They knew they would never stop that man of God from his daily times of prayer. If they could make a decree against prayer, he would be found guilty! Don't you want to be found guilty of a dedicated life of prayer! Let us be found guilty of loving our enemies. Let us be found guilty of a consecration that cannot be broken by the enticements of this world!

When the decree was signed, Daniel could have stolen away into a closet to pray. Instead of backing away, he approached his window and began to pray. He knew the supplication of Solomon many years before. *"If thy people go out to battle against their enemy, whithersoever thou shalt send them, and shall pray unto the Lord toward the city which thou hast chosen, and toward the house that I have built for thy name: then hear thou in heaven their prayer and their supplication, and maintain their cause."*

I Kings 8:44-4,5 Daniel knew the moment he turned his face toward Jerusalem, God would hear his supplication and maintain his cause. Before his enemies could go to the king, Daniel had already touched the heart of his King! While they prepared a den of lions, Daniel's God prepared an angel. What looked like Daniel's demotion became his promotion! Keep an excellent Spirit! Continue to pray on every hand. That is why an excellent Spirit was found in him. When you stay prayerful, you will always be ahead of the game!!!! *"Then said Daniel unto the king, O king, live forever, my God hath sent his angel, and hath shut the lions' mouths, that they have not hurt me: forasmuch as before him innocence was found in me; and also before thee, O king, have I done no hurt."* (Daniel 6:21-22)

"Then king Darius wrote unto all people, nations, and languages, that dwell in all the earth . . . I make a decree, That in every dominion of my kingdom men tremble and fear before the God of Daniel: for he is the living God, and steadfast forever, and his kingdom that which shall not be destroyed, and his dominion shall be even unto the end. He delivereth and rescueth, and he worketh signs and wonders in heaven and in earth, who hath delivered Daniel from the power of the lions." (Daniel 6:25-27)

In your struggles, remember while it appears you are being overwhelmed . . . God has everything under His control! When you call on the Name of the Lord . . . He hears and answers your prayer. Sometimes we are not aware of His moving until the end of the battle! Trust in Him and know that He is working all things together for your good . . . He delivers and rescues and works signs and wonders in heaven and in earth.

(Daniel 6:3) then this Daniel was preferred above the presidents and princes, because an excellent spirit was in him; and the king thought to set him over the whole realm.

The key to Daniel's splendid fidelity may be found in the statement of my text, repeated in other parts of the book, "an excellent spirit was in him."

This statement literally means that in Daniel, spirit predominated, was uppermost, and was enthroned.

We are accustomed to use the word "excellent" with other values and intentions, all of which may be right in certain connections.

For instance, we say "excellent" means fine, noble, admirable.—Yet the meaning of the word has another signification.

Excellent is something that excels, goes beyond perfection.

"A spirit that excelled was in him" That really depended upon the Spirit of God not flesh.

This is evident at the very beginning of the book of Daniel!

1. He refused to eat the kings' dainties
2. He refused to drink the kings' wine from the king's table; these are not the principal things,
3. He was a man of righteousness, his life harmonizing with God, true and the eternal. He separated himself from sin, which would separate him from God. He had strong moral character.
4. The principal thing in Daniel was not his physical appearance but the Spirit of God within him (though he was fair, ruddy, and splendid).
5. He did not change because of the ridicule he received about praying!
6. He did not respond outwardly to physical and verbal challenges to his relationship with God but continue to pray 3 times a day.
7. He didn't get angry and fly off the handle but gave all of those situations to God and allowed God to handle them.

The Church standing in the gap!

First we must understand that the church is not a building but a body of individuals each seeking God whole heartedly. In order to have a deeper life God has a further mandate for the body of Christ. We must be intercessors in the earth. God does nothing without it first being birthed through prayer. His mandate is clearly stated in the following scriptures:

Ezekiel 22:30 (New International Version)

30 "I looked for a man among them who would build up the wall and stand before me in the gap on behalf of the land so I would not have to destroy it, but I found none."

How many of you believe what God's word says in Hebrew 13:8, "Jesus Christ the same yesterday today and forever"? The Word is given to us as an example to all who have eyes to see and ears to hear what thus says the Lord! Ezekiel has been used many times to go and tell, go and speak, go and stand and proclaim, declare and believe. That is our call today! We are called to go! God spoke to Ezekiel and said go to the place called the valley of dry bones. As God revealed the vision to Ezekiel, placed the words in his mouth to speak, and brought forth the change he wants to use us in this day and time. We must hear the word of the Lord concerning God's concerns, let him show us his vision, and speak what he says in order to see a change in the earth.

Ezekiel spoke, "The hand of the LORD was upon me, and he brought me out by the Spirit of the LORD and set me in the middle of a valley" (Ezekiel 37:1-4 NIV).

The Spirit of God will lead us into some areas in life which seem unfruitful, un-necessary, and to us un-needed but he has a purpose. We must be willing to go no matter what is looks like and follow his directions. Ezekiel was focused on his relationship with God, nothing else. If God would have lead him into a furnace he would have gone, simply because his friend (the God of the universe asked him). But in this situation God had a purpose in two respects: 1) He wanted to deepen his relationship with Ezekiel 2) He wanted to bring about his purpose, which was life and multiplication.

God fostered the deepening of Ezekiel's relationship with him by leading him by his spirit to a place of purpose. He began to show him, "My spirit will take you places that are broken, destroyed, and full of sickness but I will restore, I will rebuild. If you stay close to me and listen to my voice and speak my words there will be a change." One key to note here is he was led by the spirit of God. We must be so close to God that we can discern the leading of His spirit. If we follow our desires or our vanity it will not produce God's will and purpose. When we follow our desires and vanity we create a barrier between God and us and derail his purpose. In doing this we make ourselves God, this is why God spoke, "rebellion is as the sin of witchcraft".

God led Ezekiel into the Valley of Dry Bones and he spoke, "He led me back and forth among them, and I saw a great many bones on the floor of the valley, bones that were very dry. He asked me, "Son of man, can these bones live?" God wanted to see who where Ezekiel's faith was and who he knew Him to be. He also wanted to teach him who He truly is and the power of His words. In our valleys God wants to show us our destiny, purpose, and the authority that we have as believers. Once we understand who we are, understand our purpose, understand our authority, and see God's vision for our life we will truly walk in a deeper level.

God then spoke to Ezekiel, "Prophesy to these bones and say to them, 'Dry bones, hear the word of the LORD this is what the Sovereign LORD says to these bones: I will make breath enter you, and you will come to life."

This is what we see today!

Ezekiel 22 (New International Version)

Jerusalem's Sins

1 The word of the LORD came to me: 2 "Son of man, will you judge her? Will you judge this city of bloodshed? Then confront her with all her detestable practices

3 and say: 'This is what the Sovereign LORD says: O city that brings on herself doom by shedding blood in her midst and defiles herself by making idols,

4 you have become guilty because of the blood you have shed and have become defiled by the idols you have made. You have brought your days to a close, and the end of your years has come. Therefore I will make you an object of scorn to the nations and a laughingstock to all the countries.

5 Those who are near and those who are far away will mock you, O infamous city, and full of turmoil.

6. "See how each of the princes of Israel who are in you uses his power to shed blood. 7. In you they have treated father and mother with contempt; in you they have oppressed the alien and mistreated the fatherless and the widow. 8. You have despised my holy things and desecrated my Sabbaths. 9. In you are slanderous men bent on shedding blood; in you are those who eat at the mountain shrines and commit lewd acts. 10. In you are those who dishonor their fathers' bed; in you are those who violate women during their period, when they are ceremonially unclean.

11. In you one man commits a detestable offense with his neighbor's wife, another shamefully defiles his daughter-in-law, and another violates his sister, his own father's daughter. 12. In you men accept bribes to shed blood; you take usury and excessive interest and make unjust gain from your neighbors by extortion. And you have forgotten me, declares the Sovereign LORD.

13. "'I will surely strike my hands together at the unjust gain you have made and at the blood you have shed in your midst. 14. Will your courage endure or your hands are strong in the day I deal with you? I the LORD have spoken and I will do it. 15. I will disperse you among the nations and scatter you through the countries; and I will put an end to your uncleanness. 16. When you have been defiled in the eyes of the nations, you will know that I am the LORD.'"

17. Then the word of the LORD came to me: 18. "Son of man, the house of Israel has become dross to me; all of them are the copper, tin, iron and lead left inside a furnace. They are but the dross of silver. 19. Therefore this is what the Sovereign LORD says: 'Because you have all become dross, I will gather you into Jerusalem. 20. As men gather silver, copper, iron, lead and tin into a furnace to melt it with a fiery blast, so will I gather you in my anger and my wrath and put you inside the city and melt you. 21. I will gather you and I will blow on you with my fiery wrath, and you will be melted inside her. 22. As silver is melted in a

furnace, so you will be melted inside her, and you will know that I the LORD have poured out my wrath upon you.'"

23 Again the word of the LORD came to me: 24 "Son of man, say to the land, 'You are a land that has had no rain or showers in the day of wrath.' 25 There is a conspiracy of her princes within her like a roaring lion tearing its prey; they devour people, take treasures and precious things and make many widows within her. 26 Her priests do violence to my law and profane my holy things; they do not distinguish between the holy and the common; they teach that there is no difference between the unclean and the clean; and they shut their eyes to the keeping of my Sabbaths, so that I am profaned among them.

27 Her officials within her are like wolves tearing their prey; they shed blood and kill people to make unjust gain. 28 Her prophets whitewash these deeds for them by false visions and lying divinations. They say, 'This is what the Sovereign LORD says'-when the LORD has not spoken. 29 The people of the land practice extortion and commit robbery; they oppress the poor and needy and mistreat the alien, denying them justice.

30 "I looked for a man among them who would build up the wall and stand before me in the gap on behalf of the land so I would not have to destroy it, but I found none. 31 So I will pour out my wrath on them and consume them with my fiery anger, bringing down on their own heads all they have done, declare the Sovereign LORD."

The unshakeable kingdom!

1. Devotional life (Heb. 12:28),

(Hebrews 12: 28)

Therefore, since we are receiving a kingdom that cannot be shaken, let us be thankful, and so worship God acceptably with reverence and awe, "[f]

Paul went on to teach that we should be unshakeable in our mind, heart, and soul!

2. Outreach to others (Heb. 13:1-3),

    (1). Keep on loving each other as brothers.

    (2). Do not forget to entertain strangers, for by so doing some people has entertained angels without knowing it.

    (3). Remember those in prison as if you were their fellow prisoners, and those who are mistreated as if you yourselves were suffering.

3. Marriage and family (Heb. 13:4), Marriage should be honored by all, and the marriage bed kept pure, for God will judge the adulterer and all the sexually immoral.

4. Contentment about money (Heb. 13:5),

(5) Keep your lives free from the love of money and are content with what you have, because God has said,

> "Never will I leave you;
> never will I forsake you."[

You need it and God will supply it and he will never leave you without anything!

5. Local church attachment (Heb. 13: 7),

> (7) Remember your leaders, who spoke the word of God to you. Consider the outcome of their way of life and imitate their faith.

6. Solid doctrine (13:9), (9) and Do not be carried away by all kinds of strange teachings. It is good for our hearts to be strengthened by grace, not by ceremonial foods, which are of no value to those who eat them. (10) We have an altar from which those who minister at the tabernacle have no right to eat.

7. Giving to others (13:16). (16) And do not forget to do well and to share with others, for with such sacrifices God is pleased.

In this time of crisis, check out your "alignment" in these seven areas. They will keep you stable when everything else is rocking!
Keep your mind, heart and soul connected to the heart of God the connection will keep you stable and solid when the world is falling apart!

Don't give the devil a foothold because he is your footstool!

Ephesians 4 (New International Version)

Ephesians 4

Unity in the Body of Christ

1. As a prisoner for the Lord, then, I urge you to live a life worthy of the calling you have received. **2.** Be completely humble and gentle; be patient, bearing with one another in love. **3.** Make every effort to keep the unity of the Spirit through the bond of peace. **4.** There is one body and one Spirit—just as you were called to one hope when you were called—**5.** one Lord, one faith, one baptism; **6.** one God and Father of all, who is over all and through all and in all.

7. But to each one of us grace has been given as Christ apportioned it. **8.** This is why it[a] says:

> "When he ascended on high,
> he led captives in his train
> and gave gifts to men."[b] **9.** (What does "he ascended" mean except that he also descended to the lower, earthly regions[c]? **10.** He who descended is the very one who ascended higher than all the heavens, in order to fill the whole universe.) **11.** It was he who gave some to be apostles, some to be prophets, some to be evangelists, and some to

be pastors and teachers, **12.** to prepare God's people for works of service, so that the body of Christ may be built up **13.** until we all reach unity in the faith and in the knowledge of the Son of God and become mature, attaining to the whole measure of the fullness of Christ.

14. Then we will no longer be infants, tossed back and forth by the waves, and blown here and there by every wind of teaching and by the cunning and craftiness of men in their deceitful scheming. **15.** Instead, speaking the truth in love, we will in all things grow up into him who is the Head, that is, Christ. **16.** From him the whole body, joined and held together by every supporting ligament, grows and builds itself up in love, as each part does its work.

Living as Children of Light

17. So I tell you this, and insist on it in the Lord, that you must no longer live as the Gentiles do, in the futility of their thinking. **18.** They are darkened in their understanding and separated from the life of God because of the ignorance that is in them due to the hardening of their hearts. **19.** Having lost all sensitivity, they have given themselves over to sensuality so as to indulge in every kind of impurity, with a continual lust for more.

20. You, however, did not come to know Christ that way. **21.** Surely you heard of him and were taught in him in accordance with the truth that is in Jesus. **22.** You were taught, with regard to your former way of life, to put off your old self, which is being corrupted by its deceitful desires; **23.** to be made new in the attitude of your minds; **24.** and to put on the new self, created to be like God in true righteousness and holiness.

25. Therefore each of you must put off falsehood and speak truthfully to his neighbor, for we are all members of one body. **26.** "In your anger do not sin"[d]: Do not let the sun go down while you are still angry, **27and do not give the devil a foothold. 28.** He who has been stealing must steal no longer, but must work, doing something useful with his own hands, that he may have something to share with those in need.

29. Do not let any unwholesome talk come out of your mouths, but only what is helpful for building others up according to their needs, that it may benefit those who listen. **30.** And do not grieve the Holy Spirit of God, with whom you were sealed for the day of redemption. **31.** Get rid of all bitterness, rage and anger, brawling and slander, along with every form of malice. **32.** Be kind and compassionate to one another, forgiving each other, just as in Christ God forgave you.

Maximizing Your Life!

If it was ever a time to maximize your life it is today! Now there is an encouraging word from the Lord for you in this! He said in **Isaiah 55:8-9:** "My thoughts are not your thoughts and my ways are not your ways"

We should at all times try to think the thoughts of Christ concerning who we are. God is not going to continue to tell you how to think in these days. We have to begin to train ourselves I can; yes I can no matter what the circumstances.

People are having mental breakdowns because they are having a time trying to forget how hard it is in their minds. It is not hard; it is even better for us today. We have choices, if we want to do something to better ourselves we can. If we want to settle for where we are, it is still great. But one thing I know—we are blessed.
Paul said, "I have the mind of Christ" (**1Cor. 2:16**) I am sure Paul was going through some times when something was weighing on his mind but he said I have the mind of Christ. I say to you, let this mind be also in you which was also in Christ (**Phil. 2:5**).

When we have his mind we have his views, his feelings and his thoughts and not our thoughts. But remember just because you have the mind of Christ don't think one minute that this world won't try to invade your mind with the negative things with its corruption. Be mindful of whom you are when you think. Please do not allow your mind to sink into this grave of 'can't do it world, can't have it world'. Yes! You can have it, it belongs to you and you can have peace, joy and happiness.

Don't allow your mind to wonder 'what if!' You don't have to think on those things. But think of those things that are good, lovely and of a good report!

(**Eph. 4:23**) we must be transformed in the spirit of our minds by the renewing of our minds. Keep on reading and listening to the word of God, it is the only thing that will last forever, prosper you forever and keep you.

*There are seven things we must do to maximize our lives!

1. Know that your life is hid in Christ

2. Keep assuring yourself that (**Phil. 4:13**) I can do all things through Christ who strengthens me.

3. Remember that Jesus came that you may have life and have it more abundantly

4. There is nothing too hard for God. (**Eph. 3:20**) God is able to exceedingly, abundantly above that I can think are ask according to his purpose that is working in Me.

5. The attitude we have about ourselves has a lot to do with the attitude others have about you. If you think you cannot, other will soon say you can't. That is a spirit and we need to deal with it. Don't allow you to get in your way of maximizing your life.

6. You cannot help maximize others life if you can't maximize your own. (**1Cor. 3:6-9**)

7. Learn to live long, laugh a lot, and love much

In conclusion:
Stop allowing things in this old world to get you down. Naked you came into the world and naked you will return. We can take nothing with us from this world. So, don't worry; be happy. Face each giant with the power of Faith in your heart and don't give a thought of not winning.

1. **Continue to rehearse "I am more than a conqueror" even when you are going through.**

2. **I am not going to give up.**

3. **My blessings are overtaking me.**

4. **Every time I look around, something good is coming my way.**

5. I have enough to share with others because of the overflow in my life.

6. Look in the mirror and say you are looking at a winner. Do you see that? That's you.

7. I am different and I know it. Everybody is not going to like me but they have to love me and laugh at that one just for you!!!

8. Keep on trusting in the Lord Jesus Christ, who is the author and the finisher of our faith and nothing else really matters. I f you can see it in your heart, believe it in your heart, say it with your mouth, you will run slap dab into it, no matter what you are believing God for! Can I get a witness?

Saints stay on the wall and don't come down until the work is finished and we all will see the work of God's hand in our lives for many years to come! Just be still and know that He is God!!

> The Gold is found deep beneath the surface of the ground so is the deepness of Christ! So dig in the word and you will find something better than silver and gold!

Winning over disaster!

What is the definition of winning? Winning is Victorious and bringing Victor. Winning means the act of earning a victory or succeeding in a competition. We are in competition with the enemies Strategies—Plans or methods created for the purpose!

What is the definition of disaster? Disaster is a damaging or destructive event, somebody or something unsuccessful.

There are things today which seems as though they are disastrous but in the spirit they are not, so you have to say to yourself it's just a smoke screen. If you don't you will allow the enemy to over take your faith and cause you to move too quickly and do the wrong thing. The word of God says to us! Wait upon the Lord.

Isaiah 40:31_ But those who hope in the LORD will renew their strength. They will soar on wings like eagles; they will run and not grow weary, they will walk and not be faint. Strength is the word we want to talk about here when it comes to waiting for things to get better and look better! There is a waiting period which almost seem to much and too hard to do! But the word says they that wait shall renew their strength and once they get renewed strength they shall mount up! To get onto something higher so, in order to get up higher you must first have renewed strength in which you seem to lose while dealing with the struggles of life. They can sometime become too much to deal with. But if you can over the disastrous tricks of the enemy you can over—come the felling of losing, fear, failure and weariness. Time has a very important factor the enemy always try to make everything long and drawn out so, the saints can be worn out by the time things really come to play! But use that time in which you are waiting to think on those things that are lovely and of a good report!

Philippians 4:8 Finally, brothers, whatever is true, whatever is noble, whatever is right, whatever is pure, whatever is lovely, whatever is admirable—if anything is excellent or praiseworthy—think about such things

Colossians 3:2 Set your minds on things above, not on earthly things. Some of us have been waiting on some things to happen and it seems almost impossible especially for those who believe on the Lord to make those things come to pass according to his word! It takes patience's to see the results of what God is doing in the spirit. Patience's means tolerances, and forbearance. Look at the word forbearance it means; the fact of deliberately (purposely) not doing or saying something when you could do or say it. Keep in mind the enemy wants us to speak disastrous words over our situation instead saying what the word say so keep in mind what you say is what you get. Remember the word says call those things that are not! Call those things that are NOT! **AS THOUGH THEY ARE! YOU HAVE TO CALL INTO BEING WHAT YOU WANT INSTEAD OF WHAT YOU SEE, HEAR OR FEEL!** *As it is written, I have made thee a father of many nations, before him whom he believed, even God, who quickened the dead, and called those things which be not as though they were. (Rom. 4:17)*

To quicken means—to come to life or to move in the womb. You have to Say it until you see what you want in your mind and your heart so that you will no longer say and see that which the devil wants you to see and say. See and say it until you know that what you desire has happened! Say amen, say amen I said!!! Say amen I have it now!!!!!!

You can go deeper and live a longer life a deeper life for you is awaiting! Read God's word wait and listen pray and God will increase your knowledge of him and strengthen your mind, will and emotions so that you will be able to stand in the evil days! I believe when you have finished this book your soul will cry out for more revelation of God's Word. The word satisfies a wary soul and heals the heart from fear. It take you from glory to glory a place of joy and peace!!!